WORK
AND
FAMILY
LIFE

FAMILY STUDIES TEXT SERIES

Series Editor: RICHARD J. GELLES, *University of Rhode Island*
Series Associate Editor: ALEXA A. ALBERT, *University of Rhode Island*

This series of textbooks is designed to examine topics relevant to a broad view of family studies. The series is aimed primarily at undergraduate students of family sociology and family relations, among others. Individual volumes will be useful to students in psychology, home economics, counseling, human services, social work, and other related fields. Core texts in the series cover such subjects as theory and conceptual design, research methods, family history, cross-cultural perspectives, and life course analysis. Other texts will cover traditional topics, such as dating and mate selection, parenthood, divorce and remarriage, and family power. Topics that have been receiving more recent public attention will also be dealt with, including family violence, later life families, and fatherhood.

Because of their wide range and coverage, Family Studies Texts can be used singly or collectively to supplement a standard text or to replace one. These books will be of interest to both students and professionals in a variety of disciplines.

Volumes in this series:

1. LATER LIFE FAMILIES, Timothy H. Brubaker

2. INTIMATE VIOLENCE IN FAMILIES,
   Richard J. Gelles & Claire Pedrick Cornell

3. BECOMING A PARENT, Ralph LaRossa

4. FAMILY RESEARCH METHODS, Brent C. Miller

5. PATHS TO MARRIAGE, Bernard I. Murstein

6. WORK AND FAMILY LIFE, Patricia Voydanoff

7. REMARRIAGE, Marilyn Ihinger-Tallman & Kay Pasley

Volumes planned for this series:

THEORIES OF FAMILY LIFE, David M. Klein
FAMILY POWER, Maximiliane Szinovacz
FAMILY STRESS, Pauline Boss
DIVORCE, Sharon J. Price & Patrick C. McKenry
CONCEPTUAL FRAMEWORKS FOR FAMILY STUDIES, Keith Farrington
THE SINGLE PARENT FAMILY, Alexa A. Albert
FAMILIES AND HEALTH, William Doherty & Thomas Campbell
PARENT-CHILD RELATIONSHIPS, Gary W. Peterson & Greer Litton Fox

Patricia Voydanoff

WORK AND FAMILY LIFE

FAMILY STUDIES
TEXT SERIES 6

This book is dedicated to my father and to the memory of my mother. It is they who first taught me about the joys and dilemmas of work and family life.

For information address:

SAGE Publications, Inc.
2111 West Hillcrest Drive
Newbury Park, California 91320

SAGE Publications Inc.
275 South Beverly Drive
Beverly Hills
California 90212

SAGE Publications Ltd.
28 Banner Street
London EC1Y 8QE
England

SAGE PUBLICATIONS India Pvt. Ltd.
M-32 Market
Greater Kailash I
New Delhi 110 048 India

Printed in the United States of America

Library of Congress Cataloging-in-Publication Data

Main entry under title:

Voydanoff, Patricia.
   Work and family life.

   (Family studies text series ; 6)
   Bibliography: p.
   Includes indexes.
   1. Work and family—United States.   2. Married people—Employment—United States.   I. Title.
II. Series: Family studies text series ; v. 6.
HD4904.25.V69   1987   306.8't'0973   87-9482
ISBN 0-8039-2288-4
ISBN 0-8039-2289-2 (pbk.)

Contents

Acknowledgments

I WANT TO express my appreciation to the following individuals who contributed in important ways to the completion of this book: Alexa Albert, Brenda W. Donnelly, Lora J. Durham, Richard J. Gelles, Phyllis Moen, John Scanzoni, Daniel Voydanoff, and Sandra Voydanoff. The analysis draws on some of my earlier work: "Economic Distress and Families," in the *Journal of Family Issues* (1984) and "Women's Work, Family, and Health," in K. Koziara, M. Moskow, and L. D. Tanner (eds.) *Working Women: Past, Present, Future,* 1986 IRRA Research Volume. Washington: Bureau of National Affairs (forthcoming).

CHAPTER
1

Overview

MOST OF US are workers, spouses, and parents at some time during our lives. Often we are all three at the same time. Many textbooks focus on the activities, identities, expectations, relationships with others, and responsibilities associated with being a worker; others address issues associated with being a spouse or parent. However, few texts examine work and family together to determine how they overlap and influence each other. Some recent family texts include a chapter on work and family life, but the coverage is quite limited. Texts on work and occupations have yet to address work/family issues. This book is designed to fill this gap, to deal with the complex interrelationships among work and family roles.

The lack of textbook attention to the interdependence between work and family is not surprising considering the generally held view that work and family life are separate spheres of activity. This belief that work and family operate independently of each other is referred to by Rosabeth Kanter (1977b), one of the first sociologists to examine work/family issues, as the "myth of separate worlds." The myth of separate worlds is a product of the traditional Protestant Ethic and sex-role ideology associated with industrialization. The Protestant Ethic includes the expectation that while at work individuals will "act as though" they have no other commitments or interests (Kanter, 1977b). Many individuals, including professionals and managers and those in working-class occupations, do deny connections between their work and family lives, thereby supporting the "act as though" principle (Kanter, 1977b; Piotrkowski, 1979). According to traditional sex-role ideology, men are breadwinners working outside the home to support their families and women are wives and mothers performing family duties inside the home. This ideology and the "act as though" principle contribute to the assumption that families will adapt their patterns of living to the conditions and economic rewards associated with the man's work.

Recent widespread changes affecting families have challenged the myth of separate worlds. Structural unemployment and increasingly frequent and severe recessions are taking a high toll on the quality and stability of family life. Strains and conflicts experienced by two-earner and single-parent families are becoming more apparent as these families increase in number. These changes have exposed weaknesses in the assumptions underlying the myth of separate worlds and have illuminated the connections between work and family.

Recognition of these connections has led to extensive examination of work and family linkages by social scientists in recent years. This research, much of which is reviewed in this book, clearly documents the interdependence of work and family life. The issue, then, is not whether there are linkages between work and family but the nature of the linkages and their implications for individuals, families, work organizations, and society. This book integrates what we know about the interdependence between work and family with the aim of increasing our understanding of work/family linkages and their implications.

WORK/FAMILY LINKAGES

Two general approaches are used to investigate linkages between work and family. The first, the study of direct effects, examines either the effects of work on family life or the effects of family characteristics on work. A second approach looks at how the combination of various aspects of work and family affect family life.

Direct Effects of Work on Family Life

The study of direct effects has focused mainly on documenting the impacts of work on family life. Two major aspects of work have direct effects on families: (1) the level of economic rewards associated with work and (2) the conditions associated with performing a job.

The effects of economic rewards on family life have been viewed in two ways. Most research is based on the assumption that the higher the economic rewards and the greater the occupational success, the higher the quality of family life. Joan Aldous, Marie Osmond, and Mary Hicks (1979), however, have hypothesized that marital happiness is highest among families in which the husband achieves moderate occupational success. Thus less satisfactory marital relationships will be more frequent among families in which husbands are most and least successful in their occupations. Men who are most successful have difficulty performing family roles because of the extensive effort and involvement directed toward work; those who are least successful do not have sufficient economic resources to support a family. Regardless of the specific nature of the relationship, the family's standard of living and many of its values are strongly related to the level of income derived from the employment of family members.

Several conditions associated with performing a job also influence family life. These effects, or "spillover" from work to family life, can be either positive or negative. Positive spillover involves the spread of satisfaction and stimulation at work to high levels of energy and satisfaction at home. In negative spillover, problems and stress at work drain and preoccupy the individual making it difficult to participate adequately in family life.

Work-role characteristics vary in the extent to which they result in positive or negative spillover. Moderate levels of work-role characteristics associated with psychological involvement in work, such as job satisfaction, enriching job demands, and autonomy, generally have positive effects on family life. However, at the highest levels, involvement in work is associated with a lack of participation in family life and other negative effects.

Other work-role characteristics have a negative influence on the quality of family life when they place demands and restrictions on an individual's work behavior that must be accommodated. These include the amount and scheduling of work time and job demands. Many individuals must work during certain hours at a specific place, usually outside the home. These requirements influence the amount and scheduling of time that a worker can spend with the family and the accessibility of the worker to family members while he or she is working. In addition, job demands such as physical or mental effort, role ambiguity and conflict, and time or quality pressures carry over into family life. High levels of these demands evoke negative spillover.

Direct Effects of Family Life on Work

Although the impacts may be less obvious, family life also has important effects on work. These effects derive from two major sources: (1) the influence of family responsibilities on labor force participation and (2) demands associated with various family structures, for example, two-earner families, single-parent families, and families with young children.

Family responsibilities provide an important motivation for labor-force participation and job performance among men and women. Since most men see the role of economic provider as their primary family role, having an adequate job is of crucial importance. In addition, many men moonlight or work voluntary overtime to meet the economic needs of their families. The extent and timing of women's labor force participation over the life course varies according to economic need, constraints of the husband's occupation, and the stage of the family life cycle.

The structure of the family also affects the extent to which workers find it difficult to meet the demands of work. Members of two-earner families, single-parent families, and families with young children or other dependents needing extensive care are likely to experience some problems in coordinating the demands associated with work and family responsibilities.

Joint Effects: The Work/Family Interface

The second major approach to the work/family interface, the joint effects approach, focuses on the mutual interdependence of aspects of work and family life. This interdependence operates at two levels, the economic and the individual. The economy includes two markets, the product market and the labor market (Schervish, 1985). Goods and services are produced in the product market. Families create a demand for these goods and services through consumption expenditures. These expenditures are made possible by earnings derived from production activities. Jobs are provided to family members through the labor market. Labor provided to the economy by families is rewarded by wages and other benefits. The family is responsible for its members entering the labor force with the basic skills and motivation needed to perform the jobs available. Family members are expected to make relatively large adjustments to the demands of private-sector firms regarding when and where their labor is utilized.

On the individual level, the interdependence between work and the family can be understood by examining the performance of multiple roles in three ways. First, the relationships on the economic level can be expressed more concretely through the concept of the worker-earner role (Rodman and Safilios-Rothschild, 1983). This concept makes the linkages between the economy and the family more explicit by emphasizing that two roles are performed by one individual—the worker role in the economy and the earner role in the family. In the worker role, individuals produce goods and services; the earnings from this production are used to support the family. The type of occupation and the amount of income associated with it determine the lifestyle and social status of the family.

Second, the examination of the combined effects of work-role characteristics and the demands associated with being a spouse or parent provides greater understanding of family life than looking at the effects of work characteristics alone. For example, the amount and scheduling of work time have pervasive effects on aspects of family life such as work/family conflict; however, work/family conflict also is higher among members of single-parent families and families with children.

Finally, husbands' and wives' combined work-role characteristics jointly influence the nature and quality of family life. These combined characteristics include the relative socioeconomic attainments of husbands and wives, requirements for work-related geographic mobility, the relative levels of job demands and involvement in work, and the amount and scheduling of work time. Little is known about how husbands and wives coordinate the combined demands associated with having two earners in the family or the effects of these combined demands on family life.

GENDER ROLES AND WORK/FAMILY LINKAGES

The interdependence of work and family is closely tied to expectations and responsibilities associated with gender roles. The traditional view of men as providers and women as homemakers reinforces the myth of separate worlds. The myth also is supported by limiting the definition of work to paid employment performed outside the home. Unpaid work done inside the home, usually by women, often is viewed as part of family life and not as a contribution to economic production. This view has been reflected in the social science literature in which studies of work focus on men and research on families focuses on women. Unemployment often is seen as a problem among men, whereas employment is viewed as problematic among women (Feldberg and Glenn, 1979).

An Exchange Model of Family Cohesion

A gender-based model of the joint effects of work and family on family cohesion has been developed by University of North Carolina sociologist John Scanzoni (1970). He approaches family cohesion from the perspective of reciprocity and the exchange of rights and duties. Husbands and wives exchange rights and duties on two levels: the instrumental level, that is, economic provision and household work, and the expressive level, that is, companionship, empathy, and affection. In one-earner families, the instrumental exchange involves husbands providing income while the wife takes care of the household and children. A satisfactory exchange on the instrumental level leads to exchanges on the expressive level. The mutual performance of expressive activities is associated with marital happiness and satisfaction. This satisfaction increases motivation to continue the exchanges, thereby leading to stability, solidarity, and cohesion.

Scanzoni (1982) suggests that two-earner families may be more cohesive than one-earner families because the wife's employment provides additional opportunities for instrumental exchanges between husbands and wives. The exchanges associated with wives working outside the home and husbands performing household duties increase motivation for expressive exchanges that in turn enhance marital cohesion.

This analysis challenges Talcott Parsons's (1949, 1955) earlier assumption that wife employment decreases family cohesion because it disrupts the traditional role differentiation between men and women. According to Parsons, role differentiation in which husbands perform instrumental roles—working outside the home—and wives perform expressive roles—family-related activities inside the home—prevents competition and increases cohesion. More research is needed to determine the conditions under which each approach holds. For example, families with traditional gender role norms may be more cohesive if husbands and wives perform different instrumental duties.

Scanzoni's supposition that wives' employment outside the home will be accompanied by increases in husbands' participation in family work inside the home—that is, housework and child care— also raises unanswered questions. As women increasingly have become employed outside the home, they have begun to share the duties and responsibilities of the traditional male provider role. However, men have not adopted the duties and responsibilities of women's traditional family work to the same degree as women have been sharing the provider role. This asymmetry may limit the development of increased expressive exchanges as predicted by Scanzoni.

Work, Family, and Community

Increases in wife employment and single-parent families have created a growing majority of families that have no adult in the home full time. Thus many women are less available to perform their traditional activities including child care, care of other dependents such as elderly parents, the provision of social support, and unpaid work in the community. Although most of these are viewed as family-related activities, they have important implications for the broader community. Many neighborhood, community, and church efforts to help those in need depend on the volunteer work of women and men. The need for community-based programs for the care of children, the disabled, and the elderly has grown with the increase in the number of two-earner and single-parent families. At the same time, however, the number of available volunteers is decreasing despite the efforts of many women and men to maintain their commitment to the community.

PLAN OF THE BOOK

Changing patterns of work and family life are accompanied by both benefits and constraints. This book examines these constraints and benefits and discusses their implications for individuals, families, and work organizations in contemporary society.

The next three chapters focus on relationships between major components of work roles and family life. Chapter 2 examines the economic basis of family life and the essential contributions of both men and women to the family's economic situation. The effects of several dimensions of the worker-earner role on family life are discussed in Chapter 3. Chapter 4 looks at characteristics associated with performing a job and their influence on families.

The last two chapters view the interdependence between work and family from the perspective of how the expectations, obligations, identities, and rewards of each area can be coordinated with the other. Chapter 5 examines the ways in which individuals and families coordinate work and family roles over the life course. The implications of several types of economic policy and family-oriented personnel policies for work/family role coordination are reviewed in Chapter 6.

REVIEW QUESTIONS

(1) What is the "act as though" principle?
(2) What are some of the direct effects of work on family life and, alternatively, of family life on work?
(3) How do traditional gender roles reinforce the myth of separate worlds?
(4) Is family life helped or hindered by the employment of wives outside the home?

SUGGESTED PROJECTS

(1) Examine the relationship between work and family life in the household in which you were raised. How did your family benefit from the work of family members? What negative impacts did the patterns of work have for you and others in your family?
(2) Conduct a survey of other students to find out what they expect their work and family responsibilities to be when they marry. How do men's expectations vary from those of women?

CHAPTER

2

The Economic Well-Being of Families

IN THIS CHAPTER we discuss the economic well-being of families in the context of the worker-earner role. Several aspects of the worker-earner roles of men and women are described including labor force participation, attachment to the labor force, job performance, occupational segregation and earnings, and husbands' and wives' relative contributions to family income. This is followed by a discussion of employment and income-related problems experienced by those performing the worker-earner role. Finally, we examine several unpaid contributions of family members to economic well-being.

FAMILY RESPONSIBILITY
FOR ECONOMIC PROVISION

Providing the basic means of subsistence to its members is one of the major functions of the family. In addition, families aspire to or expect to obtain economic resources beyond the subsistence level. The level of family economic well-being is dependent on both (1) the number of earners and amount of income brought into the family and (2) the needs of the family as determined by family size and composition.

Family responsibility for economic provision has important implications for family formation and for the stability and quality of family life. Couples usually coordinate the timing of marriage and career preparation and do not marry until they are able to support themselves. Young people entering occupations with long training periods and those in unstable, low-paying jobs often find it difficult to be self-supporting at an age when most people marry. In some cases those entering occupations requiring long training (for example, physicians, lawyers, and academics) marry while still in school with support from parents or spouses. Some low-income youths marry early because of pregnancy or delay marriage because of employment instability. These types of marriage among low-income youth are relatively unstable.

A minimum level of income and employment stability is necessary for family stability and cohesion (Cherlin, 1979; Furstenberg, 1974; Rodman, 1971). However, those without a stable family life lack the motivation and encouragement that a family can provide; thus the effects of frequent or chronic unemployment can be intensified by the absence of family stability (Liebow, 1967). These relationships may result in a vicious circle in which employment instability increases family instability and vice versa.

Once a family reaches a standard of living sufficient to meet its basic needs, the subjective perception of adequacy becomes relatively more important in determining happiness, cohesion, and stability (Oppenheimer, 1982; Scanzoni, 1970). Families vary in the extent to which nonessential items such as two cars, music lessons for children, or summer cottages are significant determinants of satisfaction and happiness. Most research documents that higher levels of income, with the exception of the highest levels, are associated with greater marital happiness, adjustment, and satisfaction and lower rates of marital disruption and divorce. The level of family income determines the family's standard of living and its ability to provide needed resources and opportunities to its members. Family income is an important component of social status that has pervasive influences on a family's lifestyle and position in the community. In addition, children from families with higher incomes and social status generally have higher educational aspirations and achievements and enter occupations of higher skill and prestige.

THE WORKER-EARNER ROLE
OF MEN AND WOMEN

Family members generally provide economic resources to their families by earning income through employment, that is, through performance of the worker-earner role. An individual participates in the economy as a worker producing goods and services and as an earner providing income to meet family needs. Therefore, the need to provide economic resources to the family is a powerful incentive for family members to be employed in jobs that provide adequate earnings. Although traditionally this responsibility has fallen mainly to men, it also is assumed by a majority of women.

Most married men perform the worker-earner role through paid employment unless they are disabled or temporarily unemployed. Men are expected to work from the time they leave school until they retire. In addition, they are expected to provide their families with an adequate standard of living. Both husbands and wives view the role of economic provider as a primary family responsibility of men (Cazenave, 1979; Hiller and Philliber, 1986; Hood, 1986).

Family responsibilities and needs also influence the labor force participation of other members. In the early twentieth century, the family regulated the labor force participation of its members according to economic need and family life-cycle stage (Hareven, 1977; Tilly, 1979). Families recruited their members to work in factories; in some industries whole families including children worked together in the same factory (Pleck, 1976). More recent data document that the extent and timing of women's labor force participation is still related to economic need and family composition (Elder, 1974; Oppenheimer, 1982). In addition, part-time employment among children, especially boys, was a significant response to economic deprivation during the depression of the 1930s (Elder, 1974).

Although the concept of the worker-earner role has been criticized for being used only to conceptualize and explain various dimensions and implications of men's work in relation to family life (Lupri, 1984), it is equally applicable to the work of women. George Masnick and Mary Jo Bane (1980), researchers from MIT and Harvard, discuss three revolutions associated with women's employment. Only the first, labor force participation among women, has occurred so far. The second, attachment to long-term careers, is just getting under way and the third, major contributions to family income, has yet to begin. These interrelated aspects of women's employment are basic to understanding trends and patterns in women's performance of the worker-earner role.

PARTICIPATION IN THE
WORKER-EARNER ROLE

Participation in the worker-earner role can be analyzed best by examining its major components for men and women. These include patterns of labor force participation, attachment to the labor force, job performance, occupational segregation and the earnings gap, and relative contributions to family income.

Labor Force Participation

The labor force consists of individuals who are working or looking for work. The proportion of married men in the labor force declined from 87% in 1970 to 81% in 1980. The decline has been occurring among men over 55 years of age and is attributed to the increased ability to obtain early retirement benefits and work-related disability payments and to general improvements in retirement income. Over 90% of men under 55 continue to be in the labor force (Johnson and Waldman, 1981).

The number of married women in the labor force has increased dramatically since World War II. In 1950, 23.8% of married women were in the labor force; this rate increased to 30.5% in 1960, 40.8% in 1970, and 54.3% in 1985 (see Table 2.1). Increases during the 1950s and 1960s were created mainly by older married women entering the labor force. During the 1960s, younger married women with children began working outside the home (Fox and Hesse-Biber, 1983). Until the mid-1970s wives without children under 18 had higher rates of labor force participation than mothers. Since then, however, mothers have had a higher rate; in 1985, 61% of mothers with children under 18 were in the labor force compared with 48.2% of wives without children (see Table 2.1).

Other figures document the striking increase in the labor force participation of mothers during the past 15 years. The labor force participation rate of married mothers increased from 40% in 1970 to 59% in 1984. The comparable figures for divorced mothers are 76% in 1970 and 79% in 1984 (Hayghe, 1984). The rates of women with preschool children also have been increasing rapidly. In 1985, 53.7% of mothers whose youngest child was under six were in the labor force compared with 30.3% in 1970 and 18.6% in 1960 (see Table 2.1). Between 1970 and 1985, employment rates have grown most rapidly for mothers of very young children. Rates have increased 100% for mothers of infants one year or under, 77% for mothers of two-year olds, and 60% for mothers of three-year olds. In 1985, 49% of mothers with children one year old and under were in the labor force; by the time a mother's youngest child was two years old a majority (54%) were working or looking for work (Hayghe, 1986).

TABLE 2.1: Labor Force Participation Rates of Married Women,
Husband Present, by Presence and Age of Own Children, 1950-1985

			Participation Rate		
		With No Children Under 18 Years	*With Children Under 18 Years*		
Year	*Total*		*Total*	*6 to 17 Years None Younger*	*Under 6 Years*
1950	23.8	30.3	18.4	28.3	11.9
1960	30.5	34.7	27.6	39.0	18.6
1970	40.8	42.2	39.8	49.2	30.3
1980	50.2	46.0	54.3	62.0	45.3
1985	54.3	48.2	61.0	68.1	53.7

SOURCES: Hayghe (1986) and Waldman (1983).

Attachment to the Labor Force

Figures on labor force participation provide a snapshot of the
numbers of individuals working or looking for work at a given point
in time. However, this snapshot neglects other critical information
about the extent and duration of labor force participation, that is,
attachment to the labor force. Labor force attachment refers to the
extent to which employment is full time throughout the year and
continuous over a period of years. Women's patterns of labor force
attachment are considerably more diverse than those of men.

Less than half of women aged 25 to 54 who worked during
1977 were employed full time year-round; the comparable figure
for men was three-quarters (Masnick and Bane, 1980). However,
the percentage of mothers who are working full time year-round
increased from 32% in 1970 to 35% in 1977 (Waldman et al.,
1979). Although fewer mothers of young children work full time
year-round, the rate of increase is similar for married mothers of
children ranging in age from infancy to 17 (Masnick and Bane,
1980).

Since 1965 the number of voluntary part-time workers has
increased considerably. Much of this increase has occurred among
women, especially among married women and mothers of children under 18. It has been greatest among women 18 to 44 years

of age. Some of these women work part-time during the hours their children are in school (Barrett, 1979b). Patterns of part-time employment differ among men and women. In 1985, 27% of women were employed part-time compared with 10% of men. Nearly two-thirds of male part-time workers were under 25 years of age or 65 or older; only one-third of women were in these age categories (Nardone, 1986).

Part-year and part-time employment are more likely to be attributed to unemployment by men than by women. In 1983, 70% of men aged 25 to 44 who worked part-year cited unemployment as the reason as compared with 30% of women. The comparable figures for part-time workers are 56% for men and 30% for women. These data are explained in terms of women's child-care responsibilities and men's greater concentration in cyclically sensitive occupations such as construction and durable goods manufacturing (Sehgal, 1984).

Relatively few women work continuously over their entire work history. Data from the Panel Study of Income Dynamics, a study of the work histories of 5000 families, indicate that 21% of married women aged 18 to 47 were continuously employed between 1968 and 1978. Approximately 44% were employed for 7 of the 10 years (Masnick and Bane, 1980). Young women's intermittent participation in the labor force is closely tied to childbearing. Most women leave the labor force one or more times during the childbearing years. The number and lengths of these periods vary according to the number of children and the age of the youngest child when the mother returns to work. Women having children with relatively long intervals between births are likely to experience more work interruptions. Women returning to work when their children are older will be out of the labor force for a longer period than those returning when their children are younger.

The work-life expectancies of men and women are converging. In 1977 the average man of 16 was expected to be in the labor force for 38 years; the comparable figure for women was 28 years. The average work-life duration for women has increased 12 years since 1970, whereas that of men remained nearly constant. The average man enters the labor force 3 times during his life, whereas the average woman enters 4.5 times. Men's intermittent participation in the labor force ends earlier than women's. By age 25, men are expected to enter the labor force 1.1 more times versus 2.7 additional entries for women (Smith, 1982).

Job Performance

Family responsibilities may influence work commitment and performance as well as labor force participation and attachment. It has been assumed that men with families have a stronger commitment to work, work harder, and are more stable workers than the unmarried (Hill, 1979). Data testing these assumptions are sparse. Married men are more likely to work overtime or hold more than one job. In addition, men's work hours increase with the number of children and the age of the youngest child (Smith, 1983). A recent study found that white-collar married men who are sole providers and those who have children are more involved in their work than those without these responsibilities (Gould and Werbel, 1983). Married men earn more than unmarried men even when several worker qualifications are taken into account (Hill, 1979). Part of the wage differential favoring married men can be attributed to differences in motivation and perceived need (Bartlett and Callahan, 1984).

Assumptions about the work commitment and performance of women with families differ from those for men. Married women are sometimes perceived to be less dependable, committed, and productive workers than single women or men. Rates of absenteeism and turnover, however, do not differ significantly by sex and marital status. Time-use data indicate that women spend a larger percentage of their time while at work actually working and expend greater effort at work than men do (Stafford and Duncan, 1979). Although employed married women spend fewer hours in paid employment than their husbands, their total hours in paid employment and unpaid family work are generally higher. Recent data from a national survey indicate that married men with employed wives spent an average of 10.4 hours per day in paid employment and family work in 1977. The comparable figure for employed wives is 12.6 hours (Pleck, 1983).

Although wage rates are consistently lower for women than men, they do not differ among married and unmarried women (Hill, 1979; Roos, 1983). In addition, contrary to popular perceptions, women with large numbers of children earn more than those with fewer children (Hill, 1979). These limited data suggest that family responsibilities increase married men's work hours, income, and involvement, whereas married women work harder than men and are as dependable as men and unmarried women.

Occupational Segregation and the Earnings Gap

Men and women are employed in different jobs. Women are concentrated in a relatively few occupations; a majority work in either clerical or service occupations such as beautician, waitress, and health worker. In 1981 more than two-thirds of women workers were employed as nurses, clerical workers, teachers, librarians, social workers, or in sales or service occupations (Quarm, 1984). In addition, these jobs are sex-typed as appropriate for women; other jobs performed mainly by men are sex-typed as male jobs, for example, engineers, lawyers, construction workers, mail carriers, machinists, and motor vehicle operators. When men enter occupations sex-typed as female, they tend to hold the higher-level administrative positions. For example, although only a small proportion of nurses are male, almost half of male nurses are in administrative positions (Grimm and Stern, 1974). Other female jobs such as secretary provide limited opportunities for advancement. In general, men tend to improve their occupational status over their work lives, whereas women remain at approximately the same level (Rosenfeld, 1979).

Employed women consistently earn less than men. In 1981 the median income of women employed full time, year-round was 59% that of men, down from 63% in 1956 (Barrett, 1979a; Reskin and Hartmann, 1986). Recent data indicate a slight narrowing of the gap; however, the proportion is still within the range of three-fifths (60%) to two-thirds (67%). In addition, patterns of earnings over the life course indicate that men's earnings increase substantially until they peak between the ages of 35 and 54 and then decline slowly. Women's earnings profile is flat in comparison and peaks at about age 30. This profile differs little between married and never-married women (Barrett, 1979a). Studies also show that women derive lower economic benefits from additional years of education and higher occupational status than men do (Hudis, 1976; Suter and Miller, 1973).

Why, despite recent legislation and efforts by some employers and women during the past two decades, is this earnings gap so intractable and persistent? Researchers at the University of Michigan have been studying the work and family histories of 5000 families in an attempt to answer this question (Duncan, 1984). They consider the relative importance of several possible explanations. First, they assess the extent to which women's lower earnings can be attributed to fewer skills and weaker attachment to the labor force. They report that differences in education, work experience, work continuity, self-imposed work restrictions on when and where to work, and absenteeism to care for family members account for about one-third of the wage gap between white women and white men and one-fourth of the difference between black women and white men. Among these factors, differences in amount of work experience are of greatest signficance.

Since differences in the basic qualifications of men and women leave a large percentage of the earnings gap unexplained, the researchers turned to two alternative explanations, socialization and the dynamics of the job market. The hypothesis that women earn less because they are socialized to aspire to and enter low-paying "female" occupations received little support. Women earn less than men regardless of occupation and the movement of women between typically male and female occupations is substantial.

Although men are more likely to get jobs through contacts, the "old-boy network," this advantage is not carried over into earnings differences. However, men's higher earnings are associated with the fact that men are more likely to be in positions of authority and to obtain jobs accompanied by long on-the-job training periods. Thus efforts to reduce the earnings gap must move beyond programs to improve the skills and attitudes of women workers and address components of the structure of the job market such as hiring and promotion policies.

Relative Contributions to Family Income

Most women work outside the home because they are members of two-earner families needing additional income or are the sole source of support for themselves or their children. Two-thirds of employed women are single, divorced, widowed, separated, or married to men earning less than $10,000 a year. In 1984 more than half of working wives were married to men earning less than $20,000 a year (Mortimer and Sorensen, 1984).

Two-earner familes have higher incomes than traditional one-earner families in which only the husband is employed. In 1978 the median family income for two-earner families was $22,730 compared with $18,990 for one-earner families. Women contributed more than it appears because men in two-earner families earned less than those in one-earner families—$14,900 compared with $16,000. In 1978, 5.5% of traditional one-earner families were below the poverty line; the comparable figure for two-earner families is 1.8% (Hayghe, 1981). This difference is larger in 1980; 7.2% of one-earner families were poor compared with 2.1% of two-earner families (Hayghe, 1982).

Despite the gap between men's and women's earnings, women make a substantial contribution to total family income. In 1981 working wives contributed an average of 26.7% to family income (Reskin and Hartmann, 1986). The percentage contributed varies by type of labor force participation. Those working full time year-round in 1978 contributed 40% of family income; those working full time for 27 to 49 weeks contributed 30%; and those working up to half a year full time or 1 to 52 weeks part time contributed approximately 11% (Johnson, 1980).

The effects of wives' earnings on a family's economic situation also depends upon the level of the husband's earnings. Valerie Oppenheimer (1982) suggests that wives' earnings may be an alternative to a husband's upward occupational mobility since they make a family's income comparable to that of a higher-paid occupation. Employed women whose husbands earn relatively high incomes are able to improve the relative economic status of their families. However, when husbands earn at the highest levels, most women do not earn enough to improve their family's economic situation substantially (Coser, 1985). In addition, income earned by women married to men with low earnings are used to maintain a minimal standard of living rather than to improve the family's relative economic status (Paulson, 1982).

In 1984 approximately 20% of families with children under 18 years old were maintained by one parent. Of these families 88% were maintained by women. In 1983, 60% of families maintained by women lived below the poverty level compared with 26% of one-parent families maintained by men (Norton and Glick, 1986).

The high rate of poverty among families maintained by women is related to rates of labor force participation and earnings levels. Mother-child families are less likely to have a wage earner than two-parent families. Over 90% of two-parent families have earners, whereas 69% of women maintaining families are in the labor force (Hayghe, 1984; Norton and Glick, 1986). Families maintained by women also are less likely to have more than one earner. However, even when earners are present in mother-child families, family income is lower than in other families. In 1978 the average income in mother-child families with a working mother was $8900, 40% that of two-earner families and 54% that of single-parent families headed by working fathers (Johnson, 1980).

PROBLEMS IN PERFORMING
THE WORKER-EARNER ROLE

It is clear to the casual observer that not all families are equally successful in providing a stable and secure economic base for their members. The difficulties encountered by families have two major components: (1) constraints imposed by the structure of the labor force and earnings patterns and (2) characteristics of the family and its members such as family size and composition and the number of earners.

The Changing Economy

The American economy is undergoing large-scale structural changes that will have long-term effects on the size and structure of the labor force and patterns of earnings. A recent analysis (Blakely and Shapira, 1984) concludes that the private sector is unable to provide jobs for all who need to work. The greatest shortages are occurring in relatively high-paying manufacturing jobs considered desirable by many American workers. Factors contributing to the lack of adequate job creation include the following: (1) the end of a long period of economic growth that will result in high levels of unemployment throughout the 1980s, (2) decreasing numbers of manufacturing jobs, and (3) shifts in the geographic location of jobs toward other countries, the Sunbelt, and rural areas. High-technology industries will not replace basic manufacturing industries in terms of the number of jobs provided, the levels and types of skills required, or geographic location.

Changes in earning patterns are associated with the following trends: (1) polarization of the labor force toward either high-wage or low-wage jobs, with the greatest increase in new jobs occurring in low-wage service jobs; (2) the creation of jobs derived from new technologies in industries that have no history of unionization; (3) the requesting and granting of wage concessions in several union-ized industries; and (4) the initiation of two-tier wage systems in which new employees are hired for lower pay that increases at a slower rate than that of employees hired previously.

These changes in the economy and frequent recessions in recent years are creating high levels of unemployment. Since the fall of 1982 the unemployment rate has decreased from 10.7%, the peak during the past recession, to approximately 7%. Most of this decrease had occurred by the middle of 1984; levels of unemploy-ment were relatively stable between the middle of 1984 and the middle of 1986 (Shank and Getz, 1986). Yet these levels of unem-ployment are underestimates in two ways: (1) discouraged and involuntary part-time workers are omitted and (2) monthly figures provide a one-time snapshot of the incidence of unemployment. The percentage of individuals reporting some unemployment dur-ing 1983 was more than twice the average monthly unemploy-ment rate (Sehgal, 1984).

Economic Distress

Unemployment statistics give us a picture of only one aspect of the impact of economic change and recession on individuals and families. A broader perspective emerges from the examination of economic distress, a concept referring to aspects of economic life that are potential stressors for individuals and families. Major com-ponents include employment instability, employment uncertainty, economic deprivation, and economic strain (Voydanoff, 1984a). Employment instability and economic deprivation are relatively objective factors indicating patterns of employment and changes in income over time. Employment uncertainty and economic strain are more subjective indicators of individuals' perceptions of their employment and financial situations.

Employment instability. Employment instability includes several dimensions: number of periods of employment and unemployment, duration of periods of unemployment, extent of underemployment and downward mobility, inability of youth to gain entry-level positions, and forced early retirement. At the end of June 1985 half of the unemployed had been out of work longer than 6.5 weeks; the average length of unemployment was 15.5 weeks (Shank, 1985). The difference between the two figures indicates that some of the unemployed had been out of work for a long period of time. A significant number of the unemployed experience more than one period of unemployment following job displacement (Gordus et al., 1981; Leventman, 1981). Even more workers, often a majority, become reemployed in jobs with lower skill utilization and/or income (Gordus et al., 1981; Leventman, 1981; Rayman, 1983). Of 5.1 million workers who had worked at least three years on their jobs and were displaced during the 1980-1981 and 1982-1983 recessions, about 3.1 million had become reemployed by January 1984. However, many were working in different industries and about half were earning less than they had previously (Flaim and Sehgal, 1985).

Employment uncertainty. Employment uncertainty refers to an individual's assessment of prospects for the future regarding the onset of, duration of, and recovery from unemployment. Changes in the structure of the labor force and recession-related unemployment are related to high levels of employment uncertainty among both the employed and unemployed. Many unemployed are discouraged about their prospects for reemployment; many employed are concerned about possible layoffs and cuts in income (Buss et al., 1983; Kaufman, 1982; Leventman, 1981).

Economic deprivation. The third component of economic distress, economic deprivation, includes the inability to meet current financial needs and the loss of financial resources and income over a period of time. Recession-related and structural unemployment create economic deprivation for many who previously worked at seemingly secure jobs. Others—especially minorities, young people with few job skills, and women heading families—find it difficult to get a foothold in a changing economy. In addition, economic deprivation in the form of temporary poverty results from changes in family composition such as death of a spouse or divorce, loss of a job, or illness and disability. Many of the persistent poor, such as the elderly, families headed by women, and nonelderly black men, are either unable to work or are among the working poor, those who are unable to earn sufficient wages while working (Duncan, 1984).

The extent of economic deprivation associated with unemployment varies according to prior income level, eligibility for unemployment insurance and other benefits, and the duration of unemployment. The median income of married-couple families in which one or more members had experienced unemployment during 1984 was 24% lower than that of families with no unemployment. Of married-couple families with some unemployment during 1984, 12% had incomes below the poverty level compared with 4% of families with no unemployment. Earnings in families maintained by women were decreased 39% by unemployment. Of families maintained by women, 18% were below the poverty line when no unemployment occurred; the comparable figure when a member was unemployed is 42% (Smith, 1986).

Economic strain. Economic strain is an evaluation of current financial status such as perceived financial adequacy, financial concerns and worries, adjustments to changes in one's financial situation, and one's projected financial situation. In one study of married couples economic strain is strongly related to low family income and modestly related to husbands' unemployment (Voydanoff and Donnelly, 1986b).

The Life-Cycle Squeeze

Not all families experience the same amount of economic distress; its extent varies according to characteristics such as marital status, earner status, and the number of and ages of children. Data on unemployment among individuals conceal patterns of unemployment within families. During 1982 one or more members of 32% of American households were unemployed. Another 22% had a family member experiencing a cut in hours or a reduction in take-home pay (Harris, 1982). In 1983 unemployment rates by family status and sex were 5.5% for married men, 6.0% for married women, and 10.5% for women maintaining families. Unemployment rates are consistently higher among married women than among married men. However, because married men are more likely to be employed in cyclical industries than women, this gap narrows during recessions (Klein, 1983). In 1983, 33% of families experiencing unemployment reported that no other family members were employed. Of unemployed wives, 20% had no other members working compared with 45% of married men and 80% of unemployed women maintaining families (Devens et al., 1985). During the 1975 recession, women maintaining families and heads with children under six were more likely to be unemployed 15 weeks or longer (Moen, 1979). Families maintained by women experiencing unemployment are less likely to receive unemployment insurance, more likely to receive food stamps and welfare, and more likely to have incomes below the poverty level (Schlozman, 1979).

The concept of the life-cycle squeeze provides additional insight into the interactions between income, family size, and family life-cycle stage in determining income adequacy. A life-cycle squeeze is a period in which a family's economic needs and aspirations are relatively greater than its resources. Oppenheimer (1982) has documented two life-cycle squeezes during which husbands' earnings are likely to fall short in satisfying the lifestyle aspirations of the family. These periods are early adulthood, when couples are establishing households and bearing children while husbands' earnings are still low, and later adulthood, when peak childrearing expenses associated with adolescents are not matched by sufficient increases in earnings. The early life-cycle squeeze is more severe among professionals since their incomes are relatively low in early adulthood; the later squeeze has greater impact on those in blue-collar occupations because their incomes level off relatively early.

UNPAID CONTRIBUTIONS TO FAMILY ECONOMIC WELL-BEING

Men's major contribution to their family's economic well-being has been in the realm of paid employment. Their participation in unpaid family work has consisted of helping their wives with household chores and child care and performing traditionally male tasks such as car repair and outside maintenance. Women's economic contributions have been more broadly based, including a mix of paid employment and diverse types of unpaid family work. Several types of unpaid family work make direct or indirect contributions to family economic well-being. These include housework and the care of dependents such as children, ill and disabled family members, and elderly parents; wives' participation in their husbands' work; and the management of limited resources.

Housework and Dependent Care

Women's most universal unpaid contribution to family economic well-being is family work, that is, housework and caring for dependents. Although the nature of household tasks changes with technological developments, housework remains a time-consuming activity. Full-time homemakers in 1966 spent as much time in family work as full-time homemakers in 1926, approximately 55 hours per week. Employed women spend approximately 26 hours per week in family work (Vanek, 1974). This work consists of a range of activities including food preparation, household cleaning and maintenance, clothing and linen care, shopping and managerial tasks, and caring for family members including children. Women perform a wider range of household tasks and spend a great deal more time in housework than men (Miller and Garrison, 1982). Women also assume major responsibility for the physical care and socialization of children and the care of elderly parents and ill family members. In 1977, for the first time, data show that husbands of employed women spent more time in housework and child care than husbands of nonemployed wives. The differences were 1.8 hours per week for housework and 2.7 hours per week for child care. Despite this change, employed husbands still spend half as much time as employed wives in housework and two-thirds as much time in child care activities (Pleck, 1979).

The economic value of family work is difficult to assess since it is not included in traditional measures of economic production. Two measurement approaches include (1) replacement costs, the amount it would cost to hire someone to do the work, and (2) opportunity costs, the amount of income women would earn if they did not stay home to do family work. A recent study estimates that the replacement costs of housework total more than $750 billion per year in 1976 dollars and that opportunity costs are over one-half trillion dollars per year (Peskin, 1982). Although these figures are estimates based on somewhat artificial assumptions, they illustrate the significance of family work to family economic well-being.

Wives' Participation in Their Husbands' Work

Many wives of professionals and managers participate in their husbands' careers by entertaining business associates, performing household and child-rearing tasks, attending work-related social functions, and making business contacts through volunteer work in the community. This participation is referred to as a two-person career, that is, an occupation in which the wife has well-defined duties that are an integral part of the husband's occupational role (Papanek, 1973). Occupations fitting the two-person career model include business executives, politicians, ministers, the self-employed, the military, and diplomats. Wives' participation in their husband's work is most common in situations when men work at home or use the home for business purposes, when the family lives in an institutional setting, or when wives work alongside or serve as a proxy for their husbands (Finch, 1983). This assistance provides career advantages to husbands and creates status and prestige for the family (Coser, 1985; Papanek, 1979).

Women participating in two-person careers often experience opportunity costs since many of these women do not work outside the home. Several aspects of two-person careers restrict wives' participation in the labor force: the level of economic rewards obtained by successful husbands, geographic mobility, demands on the wives' time, and lack of control over the scheduling of time (Mortimer et al., 1978). The high levels of income earned by men in two-person careers and the economic and status benefits derived from wives' participation combine to decrease the relative economic and status contributions that wives could provide to their families through their own labor force participation (Coser, 1985).

The Management of Limited Resources

Many women manage their family's limited financial resources. Lillian Rubin's well-known study, *Worlds of Pain* (1976), documents working-class wives' responsibility for stretching the moderate incomes earned by their husbands and other family members. Many of these women receive a portion of their husbands' income from which they are expected to pay all household expenses. These women develop creative approaches to cutting expenses and to raising children on limited incomes.

However, when incomes are high enough to allow some flexibility in spending, men often assume responsibility for managing the family finances. As one of Rubin's male respondents states:

> She used to handle the money. It was a pretty cut-and-dried affair then, and I didn't need to spend my time on it. But now there's more of it, and there are decisions that have to be made about what we need to buy and when we should buy it. So I do it now [Rubin, 1976: 108].

His wife sees it this way:

> Now that we're better off, he takes care of the money. When there wasn't enough, he was glad for me to do it because then he didn't have to worry about what bills to pay. As soon as we got a little more money, he started to butt in all the time [Rubin, 1976: 108].

In addition, low-income women with sole responsibility for children manage extremely limited resources through strategies such as kin-based exchange networks. As described by the anthropologist Carol Stack (1974), these women develop reciprocal exchange relationships with each other as a means of economic survival. These networks extend beyond the household to include extended kin and neighbors. Gifts of goods, money, and services made over time ensure that a woman will have resources to draw upon when she is in need. Stack provides the following example of "swapping":

> Cecil (35) lives in The Flats with his mother Willie Mae, his oldest sister and her two children, and his younger brother. Cecil's younger sister Lily lives with her mother's sister Bessie. Bessie has three children and Lily has two. Cecil and his mother have part-time jobs in a cafe and Lily's children are on aid. In July of 1970 Cecil and his mother had just put together enough money to cover their rent. Lily paid her utilities, but she did not have enough money to buy food stamps for herself and her children. Cecil and Willie Mae knew that after they paid their rent they would not have any money for food for the family. They helped out Lily by buying her food stamps, and then the two households shared meals together until Willie Mae was paid two weeks later. A week later Lily received her second ADC

check and Bessie got some spending money from her boyfriend. They gave some of this money to Cecil and Willie Mae to pay their rent, and gave Willie Mae money to cover her insurance and pay a small sum on a living room suite at the local furniture store. Willie Mae reciprocated later by buying dresses for Bessie and Lily's daughters and by caring for all the children when Bessie got a temporary job [Stack, 1974: 37].

This study documents the severe economic problems of some families maintained by women and illustrates creative coping strategies used to meet these difficulties. However, these strategies limit upward mobility for some women. When a network member receives extra resources, she is expected to share with others in need rather than use the resources to improve her own economic position.

SUMMARY

Families are economic units with the responsibility for supporting their members. Family members usually do this by engaging in a worker-earner role through which they use their skills in the production of goods or services in return for earnings for their families. Participation in the worker-earner role is the major family responsibility of men; however, in recent years increasing numbers of wives and mothers have entered the labor force. Although most women work in sex-segregated occupations with lower earnings than men, their economic contribution to the family is significant. Women also contribute to the economic well-being of their families through unpaid work of economic value, for example, housework and dependent care, participation in their husbands' work, and the management of limited resources. Changes in the economy and a shortage of jobs paying enough to support a family are creating difficulties for many families in meeting their economic responsibilities.

REVIEW QUESTIONS

(1) What economic factors influence the timing of marriage?
(2) What is meant by the worker-earner role? How does it differ for men and women in today's society?

(3) How has the worker-earner role changed over the past century?
(4) Compare patterns of labor force participation for men and women. How do they differ?
(5) What contributions to family income do men and women make in two-earner families?
(6) What are the major dimensions of economic distress? How are they interrelated?

SUGGESTED PROJECTS

(1) Trace changes in labor force participation over the past generations in your family. Approximate when, if ever, each of your parents, grandparents, and, if possible, great-grandparents entered and left the labor force. How do their work careers compare with national trends over the same years?
(2) Separately interview married couples with children concerning the time they typically spend doing housework and child care each week. How do the husbands' and wives' estimates compare with each other? Which spouse spends more time doing housework and child care?

The Worker-Earner Role and Family Life

IN THIS CHAPTER we look at the impacts of worker-earner role performance on the texture and quality of family life. We will review what is known about relationships between the worker-earner role of husbands, wives, and single parents and a broad range of family characteristics. These family dimensions include (1) family composition—family formation, stability, and size; (2) marital relationships—marital satisfaction, marital power, and division of labor; and (3) effects on children—health and well-being, child development, and childrearing. The last section discusses ways in which families cope with problems associated with performing the worker-earner role.

HUSBAND'S WORKER-EARNER ROLE

Two aspects of the worker-earner role are crucial determinants of the nature and quality of family life—labor force participation and economic distress. Since more than 90% of men under 55 are in the labor force (see Chapter 2), the major impact of men's worker-earner role performance hinges on the extent of employment stability and associated economic distress factors, that is, employment uncertainty, economic deprivation, and economic strain. The effects of economic distress on families are extensive and wide ranging.

Family Composition

In Chapter 2 we pointed out that some degree of employment stability is almost a prerequisite for family formation and stability. Without it many are unable to form families through marriage and others find themselves subject to separation and divorce. In addition, those experiencing unemployment or income loss make other adjustments in family composition such as postponing childbearing, moving in with relatives, and having relatives or boarders join the household (Fox et al., 1982).

Family composition also influences the extent of the impact of economic distress on families. Family size and composition determine the ratio of the number of dependents to potential earners available to the family. For example, families with young children must support dependents with relatively few earning resources

(Moen, 1979). Families with older children are more likely to have a mother and/or adolescents working to supplement family income (Elder, 1974). Unemployment combined with financial hardships can intensify financial problems generally associated with certain stages in the life cycle, such as that among couples with young children (Estes and Wilensky, 1978).

Marital and Family Relationships

Unemployment has negative psychological effects on individuals including lower self-esteem, lower general well-being and life satisfaction, depression, anxiety, and psychophysiological distress (Cohn, 1978; Farran and Margolis, 1983; Krause and Stryker, 1980; Liem, 1985; Perrucci et al., 1985; Powell and Driscoll, 1973; Warr, 1984). Unemployed individuals are more depressed and anxious than those who have jobs; however, the impact of unemployment does not stop here. Wives of unemployed men also experience strain and concern and in some cases anxiety and depression (Liem, 1985; Root, 1977). Unemployment is associated with lower levels of marital satisfaction, marital adjustment and communication, and harmony in family relations (Larson, 1984; Liem, 1985; Schlozman, 1979; Voydanoff and Donnelly, forthcoming). Experiencing relatively few periods of unemployment over an individual's work history is positively related to intra-family integration (Siddique, 1981).

Other components of economic distress also affect marital and family relationships. Income loss is associated with family financial disputes and marital tensions (Liker and Elder, 1983). The strain of being worried about one's financial situation is strongly related to low levels of marital/family satisfaction (Voydanoff and Donnelly, forthcoming).

The effects of unemployment and other aspects of economic distress on marital and family relationships are not uniform. Research during and since the Great Depression of the 1930s indicates that several characteristics of the family system as it was operating prior to unemployment influence the quality of family relationships during unemployment. During the depression, families operating with a high degree of unity and reciprocal functioning before unemployment remained relatively organized during unemployment, whereas previously disorganized families became more disorganized (Cavan and Ranck, 1938). Integrated and adaptable families were best able to reduce pressure toward changes in family relationships (Angell, 1936). Jeffrey Liker and Glen H. Elder, Jr. (1983), report that initially strong marital bonds reduced the impact of financial conflicts on the quality of marital relationships during the depression.

The definition of family roles and authority patterns in the family also are important contributors to variation in family reactions to unemployment (Bakke, 1940; Komarovsky, 1940; Powell and Driscoll, 1973). Robert Angell (1936) considered traditional sex-role norms to be an aspect of unadaptability in families during the depression. More recent research reports that, among couples with unemployed husbands, traditional role expectations are associated with lower levels of marital adjustment and cohesion, quality of marital communication, and satisfaction and harmony in family relations (Larson, 1984). The extent of change in authority patterns during unemployment also is related to the type of authority existing before unemployment (Anderson, 1980; Komarovsky, 1940). For example, during the depression, unemployed husbands were most likely to lose authority based on economic need or fear and least likely to lose authority based on love and respect (Komarovsky, 1940).

These relationships are sometimes complicated by the fact that while husbands are unemployed some wives remain employed and others become employed in response to their husband's unemployment. The income provided by wives is crucial to family economic well-being under these circumstances; in this respect, additional earnings contribute to positive marital and family outcomes. However, a wife's employment during her husband's unemployment also may disrupt the established division of labor in the family. In most cases, husbands do not increase their participation in family work in proportion to the difference in time spent in paid employment. In addition, both husband and wife may be uncomfortable with the husband being at home more, whether he participates in family work or not.

Effects on Children

The effects of unemployment and other aspects of economic distress on children have not been studied extensively. Research during the depression documented authority and discipline problems with children in families with unemployed fathers. Mirra Komarovksy (1940) found that fathers were more likely to lose authority with teenaged children than with their wives or younger children. Reasons for the higher loss among adolescents include lack of money to use as a means of control, changes in the fathers' behavior, and the employment of teenagers. Another study reported discipline problems including increased use of arbitrary authority by parents and children's resentment of their earner role (Bakke, 1940).

The extensive archival work of University of North Carolina sociologist Glen H. Elder, Jr., has traced the effects of income loss on children during the depression. Girls assumed more household activities and boys worked at paid jobs (Elder, 1974). More complex effects were influenced by the father's behavior. For example, the well-being of girls, especially those considered less attractive, was negatively affected by the rejecting behavior of fathers (Elder et al., 1985).

Recent studies indicate that the children of unemployed fathers have a higher risk of illness, child abuse, and infant mortality (Margolis, 1982; Steinberg et al., 1981). One study suggests that the relationship between unemployment and children's health is indirect, that is, unemployment leads to economic strain that in turn leads to parental health problems and then to children's health difficulties (Kelly et al., 1985). Children in families with employment uncertainty also have a high risk of illness (Farran and Margolis, 1983). Another recent study reports that father's unemployment, employment uncertainty, low income, and economic strain are all positively related to the number of children's problems as perceived by mothers (Voydanoff and Donnelly, 1986a).

This review indicates that men's employment instability and other aspects of economic distress have pervasive and strong effects on family life. In the next section, we see that research on women's worker-earner role focuses on different issues.

WIFE'S WORKER-EARNER ROLE

As increasing numbers of married women and mothers entered the labor force, questions were raised regarding the effects of women's outside employment on their traditional roles and responsibilities. The first studies, beginning in the late 1950s and the early 1960s, focused on the effects of mothers' employment on their children's development. In recent years, research has begun to examine the effects of women's employment on other aspects of family life. Much of this work focuses on employment per se, that is, whether a woman is employed outside the home or is a full-time homemaker.

Labor Force Participation

Family composition. Female employment is related to the postponement of marriage; however, it is not related to remaining single. Thus women who are employed tend to marry at a later age but are as likely as women without jobs to marry at some time in their lives. There is no consistent body of evidence indicating that wife employment is associated with divorce. This lack of consistency may result from the operation of two counteracting processes, the independence effect and the income effect. The independence effect refers to the idea that self-supporting working women are less likely to marry for economic reasons or to escape their parental homes. In addition, women who are unhappily married may be more likely to divorce if they can support themselves. The income effect refers to the fact that the income of working women makes some marriages possible financially and increases women's desirability as marriage partners. The likelihood of divorce may be decreased because the income provided by working wives may improve the quality of family life (Cherlin, 1979; Moore and Hofferth, 1979; Moore and Sawhill, 1984).

Complex reciprocal relationships exist between female employment and family size. Childbearing reduces labor force participation in the early stages of the work/family life cycle; however, these effects decrease as children become older. Then labor force participation begins to have a stronger influence on fertility as earlier employment and reduced fertility stimulate later employment (Cramer, 1980; Felmlee, 1984). Working women and those planning to work want and plan to have fewer children than other women (Moore et al., 1984). Research documents a complex process through which marriage at a later age, later first birth, higher educational attainment, and lower fertility are associated with labor force participation and attachment, higher-status jobs, and economic well-being (Groat et al., 1976; Hanson, 1983; Hofferth, 1984; Hofferth and Moore, 1979; Smith-Lovin and Tickamyer, 1978).

Marital relationships, power, and division of labor. Wife employment does not have straightforward effects on the marital satisfaction of husbands and wives. The level of marital satisfaction among employed wives depends on several circumstances associated with their employment. Employed wives have higher marital satisfaction than homemakers when they have high levels of education, are working out of choice, are working part-time, or receive approval and support from their husbands. Lower marital satisfaction among employed wives is associated with low incomes, working out of necessity, or holding undesirable jobs (Moore and Hofferth, 1979; Rallings and Nye, 1979).

Wife employment also has complex effects on husbands' marital satisfaction. In some cases, the husbands of employed wives are less satisfied with their marriages than the husbands of homemakers. This may be due to the disruption of routines, demands to participate in household work, or a relative loss of power and status. However, the husbands of wives who are working by choice or are working part time have higher marital satisfaction than the husbands of homemakers (Moore and Hofferth, 1979; Rallings and Nye, 1979).

Employed wives have more power in their marriages than full-time homemakers, especially in the area of financial decision making. This difference has been interpreted in terms of the resource theory of power. This theory suggests that the level of marital power is associated with the relative amounts of income, occupational prestige, contacts, and other socioeconomic resources provided by the husband and wife. Since employed wives are able to provide more of these resources than full-time homemakers, their power relative to their husbands is greater (Moore and Hofferth, 1979; Rallings and Nye, 1979).

Employed wives spend more time in family work than their husbands. Even though employed wives spend less time at work on average, they spend more total time in paid work and family work than either men or full-time homemakers. In recent years, the amount of time that husbands spend in housework and child care has increased slightly. However, since the increase is similar in families with employed wives and full-time homemakers, it can not be attributed to wife employment. Employed women spend approximately half the time in family work as full-time homemakers. Since husbands and children do not compensate for the lower amount of time spent by employed women, the families of employed wives spend less total time on family work. This difference is accounted for by lowered standards, increased efficiency, and limited outside assistance in child care (Miller and Garrison, 1982; Moore and Hofferth, 1979; Rallings and Nye, 1979; Szinovacz, 1984).

Effects on children. An early concern about the possible negative effects of an employed mother prompted extensive research on the impact of maternal employment on children in areas such as academic achievement, independence, and sex-role attitudes. This research consistently reports that maternal employment per se has no pervasive negative consequences for children. In general, the children of working mothers do well in school, have high achievement motivation, are relatively independent, and have relatively egalitarian sex-role norms. As with marital satisfaction, children's well-being varies according to conditions associated with the mother's employment. Children do better when their mothers work by choice, like their work, and provide high-quality supervision. Only one, still unexplained, negative effect of maternal employment has been consistently reported: Middle-class sons of working mothers tend to have relatively low achievement levels (Bronfenbrenner and Crouter, 1982; Hoffman, 1979; Moore and Sawhill, 1984; Moore et al., 1984).

Unemployment

Most studies of the impacts of economic distress on individuals and families are based on samples of men. The limited research on married women looks only at unemployment. These studies suggest either that women's response to unemployment is similar to that of men or that women are less negatively affected than men. Three explanations are commonly given for situations in which women have less severe psychological reactions to unemployment: less financial hardship, lower commitment to work, and satisfactions from alternative roles in the family (Cohn, 1978; Jahoda, 1982; Marshall, 1984; Nowak and Snyder, 1984; Shamir, 1985). A recent study reports that both husband and wife unemployment are related to low levels of marital/family satisfaction among men; however, among women low marital/family satisfaction is associated with husband unemployment but not wife unemployment (Voydanoff and Donnelly, forthcoming). These findings suggest that wife unemployment has negative effects on family life among husbands but not wives. More work must be done before we can adequately describe and understand the effects of wives' unemployment and other aspects of economic distress on family life.

The previous two sections have looked at the impacts of the worker-earner role of husbands and wives on family life. Now we move to an examination of the effects of the worker-earner role on family life in one-parent families.

THE WORKER-EARNER ROLE
IN ONE-PARENT FAMILIES

As noted in Chapter 2, 20% of families with children under 18 years old in 1984 were one-parent families. The number of one-parent families has doubled between 1970 and 1984. The growth rates have been relatively similar for blacks and whites. In 1970, 30% of black families with children under 18 were mother-child families; this figure had increased to nearly 50% by 1984. The comparable percentages for whites were 8% in 1970 and 15% in 1984 (Norton and Glick, 1986).

The percentage of one-parent families maintained by women has remained relatively stable—89% in 1970 and 88% in 1984. The major source of mother-child families is divorce; in 1984, 46% of mother-child families were a result of divorce. Never-married mothers constituted 20% and widows 9%. The remainder of the mothers are separated or married but living apart. Mothers in one-parent families are becoming increasingly younger because of the young average age of never-married mothers and the relatively high divorce rate among women who married at an early age (Norton and Glick, 1986).

These figures indicate the number of one-parent families with various characteristics at one point in time. However, the number of parents and children living in one-parent families during some period of their lives is substantially higher. Most never-married mothers eventually marry and most divorced parents remarry. Demographers from the U.S. Bureau of the Census, Arthur Norton and Paul Glick (1986), estimate that nearly 60% of all children born in 1986 will spend some time in a one-parent family before reaching the age of 18. Because of premarital birth, 12% will live in one-parent families; 40% will live in one-parent families because of divorce, 5% because of long-term parental separation, and 2% because of the death of a parent. A majority of children in mother-child families due to marital disruption are expected to spend at least five years in a mother-child family.

We now examine the effects of labor force participation and two dimensions of economic distress, employment instability and economic deprivation, on family life and children in one-parent families.

Labor Force Participation

Women in one-parent families are much less likely to be in the labor force than men; in 1984, 88% of men and 69% of women maintaining families were in the labor force. Except for mothers of children under three years old, single mothers had slightly higher rates of labor force participation than married mothers. The rates of labor force participation were higher among mothers of older children and divorced mothers. Divorced mothers have higher educational levels and more work experience than never-married mothers (Norton and Glick, 1986). In 1984, 78% of families maintained by women with one child had an earner compared with 43% of families with four or more children (Hayghe, 1984).

Little is known about the impacts of labor force participation on family life in one-parent families. The few existing studies are based on small nonrepresentative samples, generally middle class. Sanik and Mauldin (1986) report that employed single mothers spend less time in household tasks, recreation, and personal care than nonemployed single mothers; however, time spent in child care is comparable in both groups. A second study (Devall et al., 1986) compares middle-class families with preadolescent children that differ by family type and employment status. The findings indicate that children of divorced working mothers spend less time in out-side chores, have fewer visits from friends, have lower levels of social competence, and are more likely to serve as a confidant to their mothers than children of married working mothers. Differences in number of visits and social competence are explained by the lower incomes in divorced families rather than by family type. There are no significant differences in other household chores, number of friends, and cognitive and physical competence. These data indicate few differences between employed and nonemployed single parents; however, the data are too limited to permit any generalizations.

Other studies have considered whether one-parent families are subject to strain because no husband is present to participate in family work. One study reports that husband presence/absence is not related to family role strain among black employed mothers (Katz and Piotrkowski, 1983). Another finds that middle-class employed married mothers spend 10 more hours per week in work and family activities than single mothers. Most of this difference is due to fewer hours in home chores and child care on the part of single mothers. Married and single mothers do not differ in child-related job/family management and role strain or number of child problems reported; however, single mothers have higher levels of depression and lower life satisfaction (Burden, 1986). Once again the findings are too limited to permit firm conclusions.

Employment Instability

Although the rate of labor force participation among women in one-parent families is relatively high, levels of economic distress in these families are also high. For example, employment instability is higher among women maintaining families. In 1983 the unemployment rate for these women was 17%, twice that of women in married-couple families. A total of 23% of single mothers with preschoolers were unemployed; the comparable figure for women with school-age children was 15%. Only 9% of these unemployed women were living with a relative who was employed full time (Johnson and Waldman, 1983).

Employment status is related to economic deprivation among families maintained by women. In 1982, 88% of women maintaining families who had no earnings were living below the poverty level, whereas 29% of those with earnings were poor (Johnson and Waldman, 1983). In 1980 the median income for mothers maintaining families who were in the labor force was $11,900 for whites and $8,900 for blacks. The comparable figures for mothers not in the labor force were $5,000 for whites and $4,400 for blacks (Grossman, 1982). In 1983, 60% of families maintained by women were below the poverty line (Norton and Glick, 1986).

Economic Deprivation

A detailed study of the effects of divorce on the income and standard of living of women and their children indicates that income drops substantially following a divorce and does not increase significantly over the five years following the divorce. The drop is greatest among families beginning at higher income levels. Income in these families drops to about half its previous level, compared with two-thirds in middle-income families, and three-fourths in lower-income families (Weiss, 1984).

Income in families maintained by women derives from three major sources: earnings; private transfers such as child support; and means-tested public transfers such as welfare and food stamps. Approximately two-thirds of low-income separated and divorced mothers had earnings of their own compared with 90% of those at middle- and higher- income levels. For families with earnings, these earnings provide between two-thirds and three-quarters of household income over the five-year period following the divorce (Weiss, 1984).

Private transfers such as alimony, child support, and help from relatives generally decrease in importance over time. Among higher-income families the percentage of income from alimony and child support decreases from 40% to 25%; comparable figures for middle-income families are 25% and 11%. However, the figure for lower-income families remains relatively constant, increasing from 20% to 23%. Help from relatives is more frequent in lower- and middle-income families and changes little over time (Weiss, 1984).

Three-fourths of lower-income families receive income from welfare and food stamps; this source of income provides more than half of the income in these families over the five years following the separation or divorce. One-fourth of middle-income families receive welfare and/or food stamps during the first year; however, this figure is cut in half by the fifth year and the percentage of income provided drops from 37% to 22%. Upper-income families rarely receive public transfers (Weiss, 1984).

These changes in amount and source of income following divorce create changes in consumption patterns. During the five years following divorce, higher-income families spend substantially less on housing than before, whereas housing costs remain similar for lower- and middle-income families. Housing costs absorb a larger proportion of household income in all three groups. Reductions in food expenditures range from 20% to more than 40% and continue at these lower levels over the five-year period. Food expenditures as a proportion of household income do not vary much from before the divorce (Weiss, 1984). Thus families maintained by women experience a significant and apparently lasting decrease in their standard of living as compared with their pre-divorce status (see Duncan and Hoffman, 1985, and Weitzman, 1985, for additional data supporting this conclusion).

Effects of Economic Distress on Family Life

As with labor force participation, we know little about the effects of economic distress on family life among one-parent families. Most research on family life in one-parent families does not make distinctions by economic status. One recent study, however, looks at several indicators of economic distress in relation to social and emotional adjustment among divorced mothers (Pett and Vaughn-Cole, 1986). Respondents with higher socioeconomic status and higher and more stable incomes have higher levels of adjustment. Change in socioeconomic status since the divorce is not strongly related to postdivorce adjustment. Perceived security regarding the future availability of income and income derived from earnings or private transfers rather than public transfers also are positively associated with social and emotional adjustment. These findings support an earlier study that found relationships between the level and source of income and control of personal fate among women maintaining families (Bould, 1977). Women whose income is

derived from relatively stable and reliable sources, such as earnings, have higher levels of personal control than women depend-
ing on AFDC, child support, and other relatively unstable and
uncontrollable sources of income.

Extensive research compares family relationships and child outcomes in one-parent and two-parent families. Another body of
literature examines the effects of divorce on men, women, and
children. However, this research generally treats one-parent families as a homogeneous family type (Gongla, 1982). Little of this
work controls for economic distress variables and almost none
considers economic factors as major variables. This gap leads to
questions about the validity of this research since economic distress
is a significant determinant of the nature and quality of family life in
two-parent families (Blechman, 1982).

FAMILY COPING EFFORTS

When families encounter worker-earner problems that result
in economic distress, family members often engage in activities to
reduce distress or cope with its consequences. Coping is a process
through which individuals and families use available resources to
meet the demands of economic distress. Coping behaviors include
direct action to solve problems and the regulation of emotions and
meanings associated with economic distress. Several coping behaviors influence the extent to which economic distress has debilitating
effects on individuals and families: family work effort, participation in the informal economy, family financial management, definitional coping, and the use of social supports.

Family Work Effort

Family work effort is the pattern of participation of family members in paid employment, that is, which family members are
employed. Realigning the family work effort when a major earner
becomes unemployed or underemployed is an effective way to deal
with unemployment and prevent or reduce economic deprivation
and strain. When one family member becomes unemployed, others, especially spouses and teenage children, may increase their

work effort. Recent studies of plant closings indicate that about 20% of the time other family members, usually spouses, went to work following the closing (Rayman, 1983; Root, 1984). Although wives and children may earn less than husbands, families may approach their former income level by redistributing earnings among several family members. These shifts can lead to tension and resentment if it appears that the husband has failed as a provider or if the household division of labor is perceived to be inequitable (Kaufman, 1982; Powell and Driscoll, 1973). A recent study reports that several types of economic distress are associated with adjustment in family work effort; however, this adjustment tends to be associated with lower levels of marital/family satisfaction among men (Voydanoff and Donnelly, forthcoming).

Informal Economy

The informal economy consists of the exchange of goods and services for cash or by barter. It is used frequently by the unemployed and underemployed to reduce economic deprivation and strain. Skills developed through a hobby or on the job, such as sewing or carpentry, are used to save money or earn additional income. In some cases these activities lead to employment in a new occupation. Individuals and families also exchange goods and services such as household items, child care, and transportation. As with family work effort, the use of the informal economy is associated with economic distress and with lower marital/family satisfaction among men (Voydanoff and Donnelly, forthcoming).

Financial Management

Effective financial management, such as a consistent approach to budgeting and bill paying, is useful in dealing with economic distress. In addition, economic distress often requires sharp cuts in expenditures. Although these cuts are effective in improving a family's financial situation, they are not necessarily associated with other positive individual and family outcomes. According to a recent study (Perrucci et al., 1985), workers affected by a plant closing who report a high number of cutbacks in spending are more likely to be depressed than those reporting fewer cutbacks. A second study (Nowak and Snyder, 1984) finds that making cutbacks is related to low marital satisfaction and high family tensions among both men and women.

Definitional Coping

Several types of definitional coping can alter the meaning of economic distress and reduce its impact on individuals and families. Effective strategies include (1) individuals and family members recognizing that most unemployment is caused by economic conditions and is not the fault of the unemployed person; (2) families having a flexible approach to family roles so that unemployed husbands and fathers are valued for contributions to the family other than employment, such as housework and child care; (3) perceiving unemployment as a challenge or an opportunity to move into a different occupation; and (4) devaluing money and making positive comparisons between oneself and others (Pearlin et al., 1981; Pearlin and Schooler, 1978).

Social Supports

The use of social supports to cope with economic distress is a complex process involving several important dimensions: supports must be available, available supports must be used, and support provided must meet the needs of those receiving it. Major types of support include instrumental aid such as money, goods, and services; emotional support; and information such as advice and feedback. Support can come from several sources: friends, relatives, coworkers, neighbors, self-help groups, and human service professionals.

Studies show that the use of social supports reduces the negative impact of unemployment on individuals and families (Cobb and Kasl, 1977; Gore, 1977). One study suggests that instrumental aid, such as providing transportation for job seeking, is more helpful than emotional support such as counseling (Figueria-McDonald, 1978). Informal supports, especially family members, are considered more desirable and are used more often than support from professionals and agencies (Buss and Redburn, 1983; Gore, 1977; Rayman, 1983). Women use a relatively wide range of supports including friends and coworkers, whereas men depend more exclusively on support from spouses (Rayman, 1983). The use of family members as the major source of support may be related to a belief in self-reliance and the stigma associated with some formal programs.

SUMMARY

This chapter demonstrates pervasive impacts of the worker-earner role on family size and composition, husband-wife relationships, and children. These influences derive from the labor force participation of family members and aspects of economic distress such as unemployment and economic deprivation. The information available on these relationships varies among men, married women, and women maintaining families. The findings on men focus on the effects of economic distress, especially unemployment, on family life. Research on married women deals with the effects of labor force participation on families. Data on one-parent families establish the economic problems of families maintained by women; however, little is known about the effects of these problems on family relationships and children. The chapter closes with a discussion of ways in which individuals and families cope with problems associated with the worker-earner role. These strategies include a shift in the family work effort, participation in the informal economy, financial management techniques, definitional coping, and the use of social supports.

REVIEW QUESTIONS

(1) How does a family's composition affect its ability to withstand the problems associated with economic distress?
(2) What are some of the other factors that help to shape the impact of economic distress on family relationships?
(3) Under what conditions does the employment of wives increase marital satisfaction? Does it ever decrease marital satisfaction?
(4) Does the unemployment of husbands affect families differently than the unemployment of wives?
(5) Explain and evaluate the impact of several family coping responses to economic distress.

SUGGESTED PROJECTS

(1) Review the articles, stories, and advertisements in one issue of a popular magazine from 5, 10, 15, 20, and 25 years ago. Do you see any changes in the beliefs about the employment of men and women over time? What about their unemployment?

(2) In some ways, a group of students living together is similar to a "family." Carefully observe roommates or housemates undergoing economic distress. What sorts of coping responses are they likely to use? How different would you expect the responses of a more traditional family unit to be? Why?

CHAPTER
4

Work-Role Characteristics and Family Life

IN THE PREVIOUS two chapters we discussed the economic basis of family life and the effects on family life of performing or not performing the worker-earner role. In this chapter we move beyond employment status per se and discuss several characteristics associated with performing a job and their influence on family life. Three categories of work-role characteristics are included: (1) structural characteristics such as the timing and location of work activities; (2) psychological dimensions of work including stressful job demands, orientations toward work, and intrinsic job characteristics such as autonomy and self-direction; and (3) the combined work role characteristics of husbands and wives in two-earner families. Since the significance of these work-role characteristics varies from one occupation to another, we include occupational level in the analysis where possible.

Most of the studies done in this area have assumed that men's work-role characteristics influence their family lives and that women's family lives affect their work. Therefore, much of what we know about the effects of work-role characteristics on family life comes from studies of men. Within this context, we review the available data about the effects of work-role characteristics on family life among men and women at different occupational levels.

STRUCTURAL CHARACTERISTICS OF WORK

Recent studies show that the structural characteristics of work are related to the nature and quality of family life. Two major aspects of work, its timing and spatial location, serve as major influences on family life by determining when, where, and how much a worker can be with his or her family. This section examines the amount and scheduling of work time, geographic mobility, and work-related travel and their impacts on family life.

Amount of Work Time

Number of hours worked. In 1901 the average weekly hours for nonagricultural workers was 58.4 hours. By 1948 this average had decreased to 40.9 hours. Since then this figure has remained remarkably stable; in 1979 nonagricultural employees worked an average of 38.5 hours per week. This is down from 39.1 hours in

1968. Much of the small decrease since the end of World War II can be attributed to the growth of service industries and changes in the composition of the labor force, namely the larger proportions of women and students in the labor force (Hedges and Taylor, 1980; Owen, 1976).

Hours of work remain quite long for many workers. In 1980, 23% of full-time wage and salary workers worked more than 40 hours per week on a single job. More than 40% of managers and farm workers and more than 30% of salesworkers and transport equipment operatives worked more than 40 hours a week. Of male full-time workers, 29% worked more than 40 hours per week compared with 14% of female workers. Among those working long hours, a majority of the women work between 41 and 48 hours, whereas a majority of the men work 49 hours or more.

The extent to which one works long hours varies by family status. Married men are more likely to work extended hours than unmarried men; the reverse is true for women; that is, more unmarried women than married women work long hours (Taylor and Sekscenski, 1982). A recent study finds that fathers of young children are more likely to work long hours than other fathers. The long hours of these fathers are associated with relatively low earnings and with lower rates of employment among the mothers of young children in this study (Moen and Moorehouse, 1983). Another study suggests that permanent employment among wives is associated with modest decreases in hours worked among husbands (Mooney, 1981).

In addition, about 5% of all workers hold more than one job. Three-fourths of these multiple jobholders work more than 40 hours a week. Multiple jobholders are more likely to work 60 hours or more per week than those working long hours on single jobs. Multiple jobholding is most prevalent among professionals and managers, especially teachers; protective service workers, such as police officers, guards, and firefighters; and farmworkers. Approximately three-fourths of male multiple jobholders work at one full-time and one part-time job; half of the increasing numbers of women moonlighters hold two part-time jobs. Rates of multiple job holding have declined from 7.2% in 1969 to 5.8% in 1979 among married men. As with total work hours, multiple job holding may be changing in response to increased permanent employment among wives. A majority of moonlighters report that they work multiple jobs for financial reasons, either to meet regular expenses, pay off debts, or save for future or special purchases. Economic reasons are more prevalent among married men; men between the ages of 25 and 34; and single, divorced, separated, and widowed women (Hedges and Taylor, 1980; Taylor and Sekscenski, 1982).

In recent years, both voluntary and involuntary part-time employment have increased. The numbers of those working part time because they cannot find full-time employment moves up and down with the unemployment rate. Since the late 1960s the rate of involuntary part-time employment has been higher for women. In addition, voluntary part-time employment has been increasing rapidly among women. Voluntary part-time employment among men is most prevalent among the young and those over age 65. Among women, rates are highest among the married, especially those with children under 18 (Barrett, 1979b).

Despite the relatively long hours worked by many and the increases in voluntary part-time employment, a significant minority of workers would prefer to work more hours. Among a national sample of married men with children, 18.8% wanted to work more hours compared with 4% preferring fewer hours (Moen and Moorehouse, 1983). Another national study found that 28% of employed respondents would like to work more and earn more versus 11.3% who would like to work less and earn less (Best, 1980).

Effects on family life. Research indicates that the number of hours worked is related to the quality of family life. Several studies based on diverse samples report that those working long hours are likely to have higher levels of work/family conflict and strain, that is, respondents state that work and family life interfere with each other or that work requirements disrupt family life (Burke et al., 1980; Mortimer, 1980; Staines and Pleck, 1983; Voydanoff, 1984b; Voydanoff and Kelly, 1984). A study of 135 two-job families indicates that hours worked per week are associated with work/family role strain among both men and women; husbands' hours per week also are related to strain among wives (Keith and Schafer, 1980). Another study suggests that number of hours worked among wives is related to divorce, especially in middle-income families and in families in which the husband disapproves of his wife's working (Spitze and South, 1985). In addition, employed parents who are working overtime or moonlighting are more likely to experience perceived time shortage; working overtime also is related to job tension (Kelly and Voydanoff, 1985; Voydanoff and Kelly, 1984). However, other data do not indicate significant negative relationships between the number of hours worked and marital or family satisfaction (Piotrkowski and Crits-Christoph, 1981; Staines and Pleck, 1983; Voydanoff, 1984b). Thus hours worked seem to have a more direct connection to work/family conflict and strain than to overall satisfaction with marriage and family life.

Scheduling of Work Time

Types of work schedule. In addition to differences in the number of hours worked as just described, the scheduling of work time also varies extensively. Among the most common deviations from the 9-to-5 workday are shift work and flextime. In 1978 approximately one-sixth of full-time employees worked hours different from the typical daytime schedule. About half of these were working on the afternoon shift, for instance, 3 to 11 p.m., and about one-fifth were on the night shift, usually, 11 p.m. to 7 a.m. (Finn, 1981). Shift work is most prevalent in industries with continuous-process operations or high capital investment, for example, synthetic textile mills, pulp paper mills, industrial chemicals, petroleum refining, glass containers, basic iron and steel, and motor vehicle parts (Zalusky, 1978). In general, men are more likely than women to work non-daytime shifts; 73% of night-shift workers and 68% of afternoon-shift workers are men compared with 62% of day-shift workers. The percentage of married men and women workers is lowest for those on the afternoon shift, 60% versus two-thirds for those on day and night shifts (Hedges and Sekscenski, 1979).

A more recent variation in work schedules, flextime, involves working core hours during the middle of the day with varying beginning and ending times. The extent of flexibility varies from place to place. Some employees arrive early or work late on a regular basis; others vary their starting and quitting times on a daily basis. In 1980, 11.9% of nonfarm wage and salary workers were on flexible schedules. The percentages are higher for professionals, managers, sales workers, and transport equipment operatives. Close to one-fourth of federal public administration workers work flexible hours. Men have slightly higher rates of participation in

flextime programs than women. In addition, married men and men
with children have higher rates than married women and women
with children (Nollen, 1982).

Workers report more problems surrounding the scheduling of
their work time than the number of hours they work. One-third of
workers in a national survey conducted in 1977 reported problems
with inconvenient or excessive work hours. A total of 19% of these
problems concerned overtime or excessive hours; 27% involved a
work schedule that interfered with family life and 42% dealt with
other scheduling problems, for example, irregular or unpredictable
hours, lack of control over hours, or starting work too early or leaving too late (Quinn and Staines, 1979).

Effects on family life. Limited research suggests that these variations in work scheduling affect family life. A recent study using a
large national sample reports that individuals who work non-
daytime shifts and weekends experience higher levels of work/
family conflict. Those who work on weekends also report lower
levels of marital/family satisfaction; however, working non-daytime
shifts shows only a weak nonsignificant relationship to marital/
family satisfaction (Voydanoff, 1984b). More specific data from the
same sample reveal interesting patterns among husbands and wives
in two-earner families. For example, working weekends reduces
time spent in housework and child care among husbands but not
wives. Working non-daytime shifts is associated with high levels of
housework among both husbands and wives but is related to work/
family conflict among only husbands (Pleck and Staines, 1985).
These differences may be related to the expectation that women
perform most household and child-care duties.

More qualitative studies based on small nonrepresentative samples also suggest that shift work has negative effects on family life,
including problems with family relationships (Zalusky, 1978). Those
working the night shift are likely to have difficulty with husband-
wife relationships, whereas those working the afternoon shift have
problems with parent-child relationships (Mott et al., 1965). Jane
Hood and Susan Golden (1979) suggest, however, that the relationship between work scheduling and family relationships is complex
and that in some cases shift work can strengthen family relationships, for instance, when fathers working nights spend more time
with their preschool children during the day.

Although flextime is often considered as a way to reduce work/family conflict, information on the effects of flextime on family life is quite sparse. Detailed time logs used in a study of two government agencies reveal that workers participating in a flextime program spent more time with their children and with their spouses and children together during the flextime program than before the program began. However, time alone with spouses decreased. Most of the gain in family time was a result of going to work earlier and spending more time with family members after work (Winett and Neale, 1980). A second study reports that men spent more time in child socialization activities while working a flextime schedule than they did previously; however, they did not spend more time in child care or housework except for traditionally male activities such as car maintenance (Lee, 1983). Halcyone Bohen and Anamaria Viveros-Long (1981) have demonstrated that flextime is associated with less job/family role strain among families without children and among fathers with nonemployed wives. Flextime was least effective in reducing job/family role strain among parents with major responsibility for child care. These authors conclude that parents responsible for children need more than a slight adjustment in work schedules to reduce their job/family role strain.

These studies indicate that the amount and scheduling of work time are more strongly related to work/family conflict and strain than marital/family satisfaction and adjustment. The data are more consistent for number of hours worked than for scheduling of work time. Relationships between shift work and quality of family life are the best documented among the several components of work scheduling.

Geographic Mobility

Job-related moves and transfers. America is a geographically mobile society. Between 1980 and 1981, 17% of the population changed residences (U.S. Bureau of the Census, 1983). Estimates suggest that more than half of the moves occurring during the early 1970s were job related (Gaylord, 1979). Some job-related moves involving intercity relocation occur because individuals must move to find work; others are made to improve an individual's economic and occupational status. Individuals move to find work in response to several types of situations such as beginning a career after completing school or losing a job because of plant or office closings, cutbacks, or individual circumstances. Others change jobs and move in order to get a better job or to relocate in an area with more opportunities.

Job transfers initiated by an employer are another major source of work-related geographic mobility. In some cases an entire division or phase of operations is moved to a new location. In others, individuals are moved as part of the process of moving up the corporate ladder. Evidence of trends in corporate transfers is contradictory; some reports indicate increasing numbers, whereas others show moderate decreases (Axel, 1985; Kanigel, 1979; Margolis, 1979; Sell, 1983). It appears that transfers increased from the early 1960s until the late 1970s and then decreased somewhat. Costello (1976) suggests that increasing, though still small, numbers of executives have been refusing transfers in recent years. The main reasons for refusal include personal and family considerations and dissatisfaction with the new location. Studies with large representative samples are needed to document these trends more precisely.

Family factors interact with economic pressures and motives in relation to geographic mobility. Those in the later stages of the family life cycle and those with strong extended family orientations are less willing and less likely to move than others (Markham and Pleck, 1986; Miller, 1976). Among white men aged 30 to 39, the probability of interstate migration declines more rapidly among those who are married with children than among single men (Sandefur, 1985). Those with children under six are more likely to move than those with school-aged children (U.S. Bureau of the Census, 1983). Some suggest that the supply and demand of workers influence the extent to which noneconomic factors influence geographic mobility. When workers are in demand, they are able to give greater consideration to family and personal factors such as spouses' occupational goals, the needs of children, community activities and voluntary associations, relationships with kin and friends, and the physical and social setting (Sussman and Cogswell, 1971).

Effects on family life. The findings on the effects of geographic mobility on family life are mixed. Some studies reveal that moving is stressful for all family members (Packard, 1972; Tiger, 1974); in others, families report little difficulty adjusting to moving (Brett, 1982; Jones, 1973; McAllister et al., 1973). Since there is no uniform response to moving, it is necessary to consider the conditions under which moving is stressful. Factors influencing family adjustment include the number and timing of moves, the extent of improvement in standard of living, degree of family cohesion and integration, the availability and use of coping strategies and social supports, and the ages of children. Wives who move because their husbands change jobs have more adjustment problems when they have difficulty finding work, making new friends, or transferring their credentials and contacts (Brett and Werbel, 1980; Gaylord, 1979; Margolis, 1979; Seidenberg, 1973).

Work-Related Travel

Work-related travel is a work-role characteristic in which both time and geographic distance play a role in influencing family life. Many jobs involve frequent travel, for example, corporate manager, migratory laborer, traveling salesperson, politician, professional athlete, entertainer, construction worker, fisherman, merchant marine, and member of the military.

Most of what we know about the effects of travel on family life comes from studies of male corporate managers and the military. Managers who travel extensively have difficulty fulfilling some aspects of family roles such as companionship with spouse and children, attending family and school functions, and participating in household responsibilities (Kanter, 1977a; Renshaw, 1976; Young and Willmott, 1973). Military families generally experience longer separations than the families of corporate managers. Long separations require extensive adjustments for all family members during both separation and reunion. Several coping strategies have been found useful in adjusting to work-related travel among wives in corporate and military families, for example, maintaining family integrity, fitting into the corporate lifestyle, believing in the value of the spouse's profession, developing interpersonal relationships and social support, managing psychological tension and strain, and developing self-reliance and self-esteem (Boss et al., 1979; McCubbin et al., 1980).

This section demonstrates that diverse structural characteristics of work impact on family life. Although the effects vary according to the characteristic, occupational level, and family status, the pattern of results clearly demonstrates connections between work-role characteristics and several aspects of family life.

PSYCHOLOGICAL DIMENSIONS OF WORK

In addition to the effects of structural work-role characteristics on families, several psychological dimensions also influence the nature and quality of family life. As mentioned in Chapter 1, these influences—referred to as spillover—can be either positive or negative. Positive spillover exists when job challenges or satisfaction result in the creation of energy and enthusiasm that is carried over into family life. Negative work spillover can be of two types: (1) stress resulting from job demands and (2) overinvolvement in work due to orientations to work or intrinsic work-role characteristics.

The work of Chaya Piotrkowski, a psychologist at Yale University, shows how job demands can create positive or negative spillover among a small sample of lower-middle-class men (Piotrkowski, 1979). Workers who like their jobs and have adequate control over the demands of work bring positive energy into their families and are psychologically available to other family members when at home. Just the opposite occurs among workers with stressful jobs, for example, jobs that involve overload or conflicting demands. These workers bring their tensions home, requiring other family members to accommodate or keep their distance. Those with boring, nondemanding jobs also tend to withdraw from family interaction and activities.

Job Demands

Job demands create job stresses that may influence family relationships. Work-role characteristics associated with job stress include heavy work loads, high levels of role ambiguity and conflict, underutilization of abilities, lack of participation in decision making, health and safety hazards, the threat of unemployment and job insecurity, tight deadlines, and responsibility for the safety and well-being of others (McLean, 1979; Shostak, 1980; Sweetland, 1979). These characteristics place demands and limits on an individual's work behavior that must be accommodated; they do not imply initiative or direct involvement on the individual's part. They can consist of either too much or too little of some demands such as responsibility, challenge, or decision making. Certain occupations, such as police officer, physician, air traffic controller, and secretary, are characterized by high levels of job stress.

Data from studies using small samples find the following job demands related to work/family conflict and family role strain: role ambiguity, role conflict, intellectual and physical effort, rapid change, pressures for quality work, and a heavy work load (Burke et al., 1980; Jones and Butler, 1980; Katz and Piotrkowski, 1983). In a national study that assesses the relative importance of several job demands in relation to family life, job pressure is of greatest importance in relation to work/family conflict followed by ambiguity and role conflict. Job insecurity made no contribution to work/family conflict; however, it was the only job demand associated with lower levels of marital/family satisfaction (Voydanoff, 1984b).

Orientations to Work

Other characteristics associated with jobs, orientations to work and intrinsic work-role characteristics, also spill over into family life. These characteristics are more likely to engender positive spillover than job demands, especially when present at moderate levels. Two major orientations to work are significant in relation to quality of family life—job involvement and job satisfaction.

Job involvement. Involvement in the work role is higher among those in high-status occupations, for example, professionals and managers. Joseph Pleck and Linda Lang (1978) report that only a highly educated minority of their national sample show greater involvement in work than in family roles. A second study, using a small sample of men in England, finds higher levels of work/family interference, thinking of work while at home, and feeling pressed at home among professionals and managers (Young and Willmott, 1973). This pattern is accentuated when those at the highest level, managing directors, are compared with other professionals and managers.

Young and Willmott (1973: 166-167) provide the following examples of job involvement among managers:

> I think about work continually when I'm at home. If you are digging a flower bed for a couple of hours you can have a marvellous think about some deep problems of organization. You are not necessarily trying to think something through at high pressure; you are just mulling it over.

> When I'm in the bath or mowing the lawn, I'm often trying to figure out some problem or other. It's happening all the time.

> If you saw me very happily sitting in the garden with a drink at my side I might be thinking over a problem. If you came along beside me you might be talking to me for ten minutes and I wouldn't hear you, I'd be so concentrated. There is a total commitment to my job. I'd almost say that my work is my leisure.

> I think work does interfere at home. Possibly in my manner. You get drawn down sometimes when you've got problems inside you. It makes you a little more difficult to get on with at home.

> One has problems. You think about them and drift into a haze and don't pay attention to what your wife is telling you. I said that I never take work home—that's true, not paper work. But unfortunately it remains in my head. There are the usual domestic problems as a result.

Among male professionals and managers, high job involvement is related to high levels of work/family conflict and low levels of marital satisfaction (Greenhaus and Kopelman, 1981; Mortimer, 1980; Voydanoff, 1982). Other studies report higher levels of marital satisfaction and couple enjoyment of activities among college-educated couples in which the husband and/or wife is family-oriented rather than work-oriented (Bailyn, 1970; Rapoport et al., 1974).

Two studies of male workers indicate that the extent to which job involvement and job stress affect family life depends on how much a worker's spouse supports him in his work. Jeylan Mortimer (1980) found that job involvement among professionals and managers is associated with low levels of marital satisfaction except for those who indicate that their wives support their occupational efforts. Wife support serves as a mediating variable since job involvement is positively related to wife support, which in turn is positively related to marital satisfaction. A second study reports that satisfaction with the husband-wife helping relationship serves as an effective mediator between job and life stress and several measures of well-being including job, marital, and life satisfaction and mental and physical well-being (Burke and Weir, 1975, 1977).

Job satisfaction. Less is known about the effects of job satisfaction on family life. A national study of male professionals and managers found that high levels of job satisfaction are associated with low levels of work/family conflict and high levels of marital/family satisfaction (Voydanoff, 1982). In addition, high levels of job satisfaction are related to low levels of perceived time shortage and job tension among a sample of working parents (Kelly and Voydanoff, 1985; Voydanoff and Kelly, 1984). However, job satisfaction is not related to family role strain among a small nonrepresentative sample of employed black women (Katz and Piotrkowski, 1983).

Thus job satisfaction has more positive effects on family life than job involvement. Perhaps the positive attitudes associated with job satisfaction spill over into family life, whereas preoccupation associated with job involvement distracts from family life.

Intrinsic Work-Role Characteristics

Intrinsic work-role characteristics focus on the content of a job, for example, extent of challenge, autonomy, and self-direction. The findings relating intrinsic characteristics to family life are limited. One study found that high levels of job challenge and job variety are associated with low levels of family/work role incompatibility among married sailors (Jones and Butler, 1980). Another reports that intrinsic job gratification is related to positive family relations among high-status, but not lower-status, women (Piotrkowski and Crits-Christoph, 1981). Finally, in a study using a national sample, enriching job demands are associated with high levels of marital satisfaction; however, they are not related to work/family conflict (Voydanoff, 1984b).

The findings on autonomy are contradictory. One study reports that job autonomy is associated with higher levels of family/work role incompatibility (Jones and Butler, 1980), whereas another finds that autonomy is associated with lower levels of family role strain (Katz and Piotrkowski, 1983). A third study (Burke et al., 1980) found no relationship between autonomy and family/work role incompatibility. In a national sample, autonomy is associated with lower levels of work/family conflict and higher levels of marital/family satisfaction (Voydanoff, 1984b). The bulk of the evidence based on large representative samples suggests that intrinsic characteristics are associated with low work/family conflict and high satisfaction.

Another intrinsic work-role characteristic, self-direction in work, has been studied extensively by Melvin Kohn and his colleagues (Kohn, 1977; Kohn and Schooler, 1983). Kohn's initial aim was to explain class differences in parents' values for their children and childrearing techniques. He noted that middle-class and working-class parents differ in the extent to which they emphasize self-direction and conformity as major values for their children. Middle-class parents emphasize self-direction by teaching responsibility, self-control, and an interest in how and why things happen. Working-class parents are likely to instill values such as obedience, neatness and cleanliness, and honesty.

Kohn finds that the conditions associated with middle-class and working-class occupations explain the class differences in parental values and practices. Self-direction characterizes middle-class occupations, whereas conformity to external authority is more prevalent in working-class occupations. Workers use the conditions they deal with at work as a reference for the values they think their children should learn so that they can make their way in the world. This research indicates that the degree of occupational self-direction influences parental values and childrearing practices and documents that occupational conditions affect the values and behavior of other family members. Kohn's research focuses on men; however, other studies reveal that similar occupational conditions influence the job satisfaction, intellectual functioning, and social orientation of women in much the same way as they affect men (Miller, 1980; Miller et al., 1979).

JOINT EFFECTS OF HUSBANDS' AND WIVES' WORK-ROLE CHARACTERISTICS ON FAMILY LIFE

So far we have discussed the effects of the work-role characteristics of one individual on his or her family life. This section looks at the effects of husbands' and wives' combined work-role characteristics on family life among two-earner and two-career families. Three major aspects of husbands' and wives' combined work characteristics are related to the nature and quality of family life: relative socioeconomic attainment of husbands and wives, work-related geographic mobility and commuter marriage, and amount and scheduling of work time.

Relative Socioeconomic Attainment of Husbands and Wives

Many people believe that families in which wives are more successful than their husbands are plagued with difficulties. Unfortunately, we have little data bearing on this issue. However, the limited data that are available suggest that wives' relative success has negative effects on the quality of family life. For example, achievement-oriented men whose wives have high levels of education in relation to their own report low levels of marital satisfaction (Hornung and McCullough, 1981). However, women whose husbands have relatively high levels of education report higher levels of marital satisfaction. In addition, husbands, but not wives, have low marital satisfaction when the wife's occupation is higher than expected based on the husband's level of education. In a second study, based on a different sample, the likelihood of life-threatening family violence is higher among couples in which the wife's occupation is relatively high in comparison with her husband's occupation (Hornung et al., 1981).

A third study suggests that other occupational factors also are important in relation to quality of family life. William Philliber and Dana Hiller (1983) found that women employed in nontraditional occupations in 1967 were more likely to have divorced, to have left the labor force, or to have shifted to a lower status position by 1974 than women in traditional occupations in 1967. Being employed in a nontraditional occupation was more strongly related to these changes than the relative occupational status of the husband and wife.

Work-Related Geographic Mobility and Commuter Marriage

As we discussed earlier, work-related moves can create problems within families. These moves become more complicated when they involve two-career or two-earner families. A few small-scale studies of this issue indicate that, although some husbands are refusing transfers and new job opportunities because of their wives' careers, the effects of work-related moves are greater for women than men. Women are much more likely to move to accommodate their spouses' job changes and transfers than men (Duncan and Perrucci, 1976; Foster et al., 1980; Spitze, 1986). Such moves negatively affect wives' employment status, weeks worked, and earnings; however, limited research suggests that these effects have disappeared two years after the move (Lichter, 1983; Spitze, 1984).

A recent alternative to one spouse moving to accommodate the career of the other is a commuter marriage in which spouses work in different locations during the week and reunite on weekends. This type of marriage differs from that in which men in one-earner families are frequently away from home for work-related purposes, for example, among merchant marines, entertainers, athletes, politicians, and the military. In commuter marriages, neither occupation may require frequent travel; instead, the two jobs are in locations too distant to allow daily commuting from one home. The success of commuter marriages depends upon several family and work characteristics. Commuter marriages are more successful when the two jobs are located relatively close to each other, the separations are of short duration, both spouses are strongly career-oriented, at least one spouse has an established career, and the couples are older, married longer, and free from childrearing responsibilities (Gerstel and Gross, 1984).

Amount and Scheduling of Work Time

We are just beginning to get information about how the total hours worked by husbands and wives affect family life. Data from a national survey indicate that marital satisfaction is highest among couples in which the husband works full time or longer and the wife works part time (reduced hours) and is lowest for couples in which both husband and wife work at least full-time and one or both work overtime or hold second jobs (extended hours). Working reduced hours is associated with the lowest levels of work/family conflict for women and the highest levels for men (Dempster-McClain and

Moen, 1983). Perhaps working reduced hours facilitates the performance of household duties among women and is accompanied by higher household demands among men. A second analysis of the same national survey data finds that a high total number of hours worked by a couple is associated with spending less time with children and lower family satisfaction for both men and women and to work/family conflict among women; however, total hours are not related to marital happiness or satisfaction (Kingston and Nock, 1985).

Paul Kingston and Steven Nock (1985) have developed a measure of the length of the family workday, that is, the total number of hours that at least one spouse is at work, in order to examine the joint effects of the husband's and wife's work schedules on family life. Women reporting a long family workday spend more time on chores and less free time with their spouses. A long family workday is related to higher family satisfaction among men. However, the length of the family workday is not related to marital happiness or satisfaction. A third analysis of these national survey data reveals that the relationships between husbands' non-daytime and variable shifts and schedule conflicts with the family are stronger when wives also work non-daytime or variable shifts (Staines and Pleck, 1983).

These studies of the effects of combined husband-wife work characteristics on family life reveal diverse effects. However, because research of this type is in its infancy, it is impossible to draw firm conclusions regarding the nature and extent of these effects.

SUMMARY

Several characteristics associated with performing a job affect family life. Structural characteristics such as amount and scheduling of work time and work-related travel influence the amount of time a worker is available to the family. Work-related geographic mobility determines the family's community of residence and its closeness to the extended family.

Other work-role characteristics are associated with the psychological spillover from work to family. Several job demands may induce job stress that has negative effects on family relationships. Other work-role characteristics can create positive spillover into family life. Some of these positive characteristics, such as job involvement and satisfaction, may have more beneficial effects at moderate rather than very high or low levels.

As the number of two-earner families has increased, the need to understand the effects of combined husband-wife work-role characteristics on family life has become more apparent. Preliminary studies indicate that, despite their complexity, the effects of these combined characteristics are important enough to warrant further study.

REVIEW QUESTIONS

(1) Compare the impact of working long hours on the family lives of men and women.
(2) How is working weekends and non-daytime shifts tied to the quality of family life?
(3) How are job demands related to the quality of family life?
(4) Explain what is meant by intrinsic work-role characteristics.
(5) How do husbands' and wives' work-role characteristics combine to influence family life?

SUGGESTED PROJECTS

(1) Consider whether flextime programs are likely to make an impact on the quality of family life. Why or why not?
(2) Describe work-role characteristics that most likely would strengthen the quality of family life. Then, present a worst-case scenario; a family with work-role characteristics consistently associated with negative effects on the quality of family life.

CHAPTER
5

Individual Work/Family Role Coordination

PREVIOUS CHAPTERS HAVE addressed the direct effects of family structure demands on work and of labor force participation, economic
distress, and work-role characteristics on family life. This chapter
examines the constraints and rewards associated with performing
both work and family roles and the mechanisms individuals use to
coordinate the demands associated with work and family activities.
The interdependence of work and family careers is illustrated by
the concept of the work/family life cycle, which provides a means
for mapping the increasing variety of ways in which men and
women coordinate work and family roles over the life course.
Three major means of coordinating work and family roles—the
use of coping strategies, sequential work/family role staging, and
symmetrical work/family role allocation, also are discussed.

MULTIPLE ROLES, ROLE STRAIN, AND ROLE EXPANSION

Most individuals at some time perform the roles of worker,
parent, and spouse; often all are performed simultaneously. The
demands and rewards associated with performing multiple roles
can be analyzed in terms of role accumulation. Role accumulation
is defined as the total number of roles in an individual's role set
(Burr et al., 1979). Work and family roles such as worker, spouse,
parent, and relative involve activities, identities, obligations, rewards,
and relationships with diverse others.

There is disagreement as to whether performing multiple roles
results in role strain. The well-known sociologist William J. Goode
defines role strain as "the felt difficulty in performing role obligations." (Goode, 1960: 483). He asserts that "the individual is likely
to face a wide, distracting, and sometimes conflicting array of role
obligations. If he conforms fully or adequately in one direction, ful-
fillment will be difficult in another. . . . In general, *the individual's
total role obligations are overdemanding*," and, therefore, role strain
is normal (Goode, 1960: 485). Burr et al. (1979) hypothesize that
the greater the role accumulation, the greater the perceived role
incompatibility and the greater the role strain.

Others suggest that role strain theory emphasizes the demands
associated with roles to the neglect of rewards and privileges. Sam
Sieber (1974) proposes that the following rewards are associated
with role accumulation: role privileges that can assist in the man-

agement of multiple roles; role perquisites that provide status enhancement and facilitate role performance; status security in which success in one role can compensate for failure in another; and personality enrichment and ego gratification. Sieber argues that these rewards outweigh the negative effects of role accumulation.

A third approach to role strain theory is the expansion approach that Stephen Marks (1977) uses to explain why some individuals performing multiple roles experience role strain while others do not. Marks argues that under certain conditions multiple roles result in energy creation rather than depletion. He sees the relative degree of commitment to various roles as a critical determinant of role strain. When all commitments have equally positive or negative value, role strain will not occur. However, when there is variation in the level of positive commitment to different roles, the energy and time allocated for overcommitted interests expands and encroaches on the time and energy available for the undercommitted interests. In this situation, scarcity arguments are used to excuse a lack of participation in undercommitted interests. The relative priority assigned to different roles is influenced by cultural priorities; for example, work is often an overcommitted interest among middle-class men.

A somewhat different approach to understanding positive effects of performing multiple roles is put forward by the Princeton University sociologist Peggy Thoits (1983). Her identity accumulation hypothesis posits that multiple roles are accompanied by multiple identities that are associated with lower levels of psychological distress. She argues that "social identities provide actors with existential meaning and behavioral guidance, and that these qualities are essential to psychological well-being and organized, functional behavior" (Thoits, 1983: 183). She presents data showing that the number of identities and increases in the number of identities over time are associated with lower levels of psychological distress.

THE EFFECTS OF MULTIPLE
ROLES ON WOMEN'S LIVES

Almost all studies of the combined effects of performing work and family roles are based on samples of women. According to Marks's (1977) approach, men are overcommitted to work and make scarcity excuses to limit their family role participation. This overcommitment to work and undercommitment to family has been culturally accepted and therefore not considered an issue needing study. However, since women are increasing their relative commitment to work outside the home, thereby changing their balance of commitments, the issue of the effects of multiple roles is salient. As mentioned earlier, labor force participation by women has been considered by many to be harmful and disruptive to family life. A similar argument has been made regarding the joint effects of work and family roles on women's physical and mental health and on the quality of their family lives. Let us now consider the empirical evidence regarding the effects of women's multiple roles on health and family life.

Effects of Women's Multiple Roles on Family Life

The few studies that examine the joint effects of work-role characteristics and family demands on quality of family life among women reveal that both work and family characteristics are related to perceived work/family conflict (Cooke and Rousseau, 1984; Katz and Piotrkowski, 1983; Keith and Schafer, 1980). These variables include work hours, job involvement, job autonomy, time expectations at work, marital status, and number and ages of children. A study of working parents reports that family demands— presence of school-age children—explain more variance in perceived time shortage, whereas work-role characteristics—dissatisfaction with job duties, hours, and schedule—explain more variance in job tension (Kelly and Voydanoff, 1985; Voydanoff and Kelly, 1984). The most extensive study including both work and family characteristics indicates that work-role characteristics and family structure demands have additive effects on work/family conflict and marital/ family satisfaction; that is, each characteristic makes an independent contribution to quality of family life (Voydanoff, 1984b). Work-role characteristics and family demands do not have interactive effects in which work-role characteristics exacerbate the effects of family demands on family life or vice versa.

Effects of Women's Multiple Roles on Physical Health

Several studies have examined the combined effects of work and family roles on women's physical health. The University of Michigan researcher Lois Verbrugge (1983) reports that being employed, married, and a parent show independent positive relationships with physical health outcomes. Health levels are highest among women performing all three roles, whereas those performing none have the poorest health; these relationships are additive, not interactive. A second study reports both positive main effects for marital status, children, and employment and significant positive interactions indicating better health for women who combine employment and children and women who are married with children (Nathanson, 1980).

In apparent contrast, Nancy Woods and Barbara Hulka (1979) find that higher numbers of role responsibilities are associated with physical health symptoms. Having three or more children or an ill spouse show the strongest relationships. Another study reports high rates of coronary heart disease among clerical workers and women with three or more children. These rates are especially high among married clerical workers with children (Haynes and Feinleib, 1980). Thus, although performing multiple roles is generally associated with good physical health, specific combinations of work and family roles are negatively related to health.

Verbrugge (1985) presents a more detailed analysis of the combined effects of work-role characteristics and family demands on health. She finds poor health related to several role burdens including irregular or short work schedules, dissatisfaction with work and other major roles, few or many time constraints, few or many family dependents, and few role involvements and responsibilities. She suggests that poor health is associated with few responsibilities because unhealthy individuals are unable to engage in as many activities as the healthy; on the other hand, high levels of responsibility are related to poor health because of the stress associated with high demands.

Effects of Women's Multiple Roles on Mental Health

Studies of relationships among work, family, and mental health reveal findings similar to those for physical health. Women who are married, are employed outside the home, or are mothers have lower levels of depression (Aneshensel et al., 1982; Gore and Mangione, 1983; Kandel et al., 1985). Married and employed women also report fewer psychophysiological complaints; however, having minor children at home is associated with more complaints (Gore and Mangione, 1983).

The analysis of the performance of multiple roles yields complex results. A recent study reports that women who are married, working, and parents have the lowest levels of depression, whereas those who are single, not working, and not parents have the highest levels (Kandel et at., 1985). Other data reveal interactions among the three roles in relation to depression. For example, Cleary and Mechanic (1983) find that marital status is less strongly related to depression among employed women than among homemakers. However, having children at home is positively related to depression among employed women. Another study indicates that psychiatric symptoms increase with the number of children among employed women but not among homemakers (Gove and Geerken, 1977).

Our understanding of the impact of multiple roles on mental health can be improved by looking at the effects of stress associated with performing work and family roles. A recent study finds that employment role strain and marital role strain are associated with depression (Aneshensel, 1986). A second study reports that being employed buffers the effects of marital stress on depression, whereas parenthood exacerbates the effects of occupational stress (Kandel et al., 1985).

This research reveals several types of relationship among women's work and family roles, quality of family life, and mental and physical health. The number of roles performed is positively related to health. Several characteristics associated with performing work and family roles also show direct relationships to family life and health. In addition, various combinations of work and family-role characteristics have diverse effects on health and family life.

COPING WITH ROLE CONFLICT

Overload and Interference

Role strain theory suggests two major types of role conflict resulting from performing multiple roles: overload and interference.

Overload exists when the total demands on time and energy associated with the prescribed activities of multiple roles are too great to perform the roles adequately or comfortably. Interference occurs when conflicting demands make it difficult to fulfill the requirements of multiple roles. Interference is of two major types. First, role expectations may be contradictory or there may be a lack of consensus regarding expectations. The expectations of one role may conflict with those of another. The second type, role incompatibility, is the inability to perform the prescribed activities for both roles because of conflicts in the scheduling of demands. Many activities must be performed in specific locations at specific times.

Coping Strategies

Within the context of structural constraints, individuals manipulate the demands associated with their multiple roles in order to construct workable patterns of relationships and activities. Two major techniques are used: (1) manipulation of the person's role structure and relationships and (2) the negotiation of the terms of relationships with others involved in a role (Goode, 1960). Goode (1960) identifies the following techniques of role manipulation: (1) compartmentalization of role obligations; (2) delegation of role obligations; (3) elimination of role relationships; (4) extension of role relationships, that is, adding roles to provide scarcity excuses or to facilitate role performance; and (5) the creation of barriers against intrusion from role partners. The technique of role extension is similar to the approach discussed by Sieber (1974) in which individuals use the rewards from one role to facilitate performance in another role. For example, personal and family contacts, recommendations, and invitations to social gatherings can be useful in advancing one's career. The second approach, negotiating the terms of relationships with others involved in the role, includes role-bargaining techniques. Role bargaining determines the standards by which the quality of role performance is evaluated. Husbands and wives negotiate the criteria by which the success of work outside and inside the home is evaluated.

Empirical research on coping strategies to deal with overload and interference resulting from performing work and family roles has been very limited. The few existing studies examine small nonrepresentative samples of college-educated women or women in two-career families. Much of this research is based on a categorization of coping strategies developed by the Yale University psychologist Douglas Hall (1972). His model consists of three major approaches to coping: (1) structural role redefinition, similar to Goode's role-bargaining process, which includes strategies such as obtaining role supports from inside and outside the role set, problem solving in role relationships, and changing societal definitions of roles; (2) personal role redefinition, which includes eliminating roles, establishing priorities, compartmentalizing role demands, and changing one's attitudes toward roles; and (3) reactive role behavior, which includes planning, scheduling, organizing, working harder, and having a passive orientation to demands.

Margaret Elman and Lucia Gilbert (1984) extend this model by using the distinction between problem-focused and emotion-focused coping strategies. Problem-focused strategies, such as the types proposed by Hall, are oriented toward managing or eliminating multiple role conflict. Emotion-focused strategies include cognitive restructuring, for example, deciding that areas of stress are not important, and tension reduction techniques. These strategies focus on modifying an individual's emotional reaction to role conflict.

The small-scale studies conducted so far do not present conclusive results regarding the relative effectiveness of these coping strategies for reducing role conflict or increasing satisfaction with roles and role performance. Hall's (1972) findings indicate that structural and personal role redefinition are associated with high levels of career satisfaction, whereas reactive role behavior is related to low satisfaction. Algea Harrison and Joanne Minor (1978) report a relationship between the type of conflict and the type of coping strategy used. Wife-mother conflict is most often dealt with through structural role redefinition; mother-worker conflict through personal role redefinition; and mother-wife conflict through either structural or personal redefinition. However, the choice of coping strategy is not related to satisfaction with role performance. Nicholas Beutell and Jeffrey Greenhaus (1983) found that women with traditional sex-role attitudes were more likely to use reactive role behavior; however, this behavior is not perceived to be as successful in resolving home-non-home conflict as other approaches. Elman and Gilbert (1984) report that increased role behavior (organizing, planning, and working harder), cognitive restructuring, and personal role redefinition are the most frequently used coping strategies among mothers of preschool children in two-career families. Increased role behavior and cognitive restructuring are significantly related to perceived coping effectiveness. These initial studies have mapped out some important issues and provided leads for future research in this area.

THE WORK/FAMILY LIFE CYCLE

Another approach to understanding the conditions under which performing multiple work and family roles is associated with overload and interference examines the nature of work and family roles over the life course. Both work and family careers consist of stages that vary according to developmental tasks over the life course. These stages encompass different forms of relationships characterized by differing demands, expectations, identities, histories, and projected futures. The stages in these two careers intersect to form the work/family life cycle.

Stages in the Family Career

The family life cycle or family career is a major concept in the family development framework. The family career consists of several stages, each of which is characterized by specific developmental tasks to be accomplished. These tasks include physical maintenance, socialization, motivation to perform roles, social control, and addition and release of family members (Aldous, 1978). Family career stages are mapped out in several ways according to family size and composition, marital status, ages and school placement of children, and the employment status of major wage earners. This analysis uses the following stages based on the work of Reuben Hill (1964), one of the original creators of the family development framework:

(I) Establishment—newly married couples without children.
(II) New Parents—couples with infants or children under school age.
(III) School Age Family—couples with school-age children.

(IV) Postparental Family—couples after children have left home and/ or entered the productive sector.

(V) Aging Family—couples after retirement.

This conceptualization of the family career assumes a long-standing husband-wife relationship accompanied by the parenting of one or more children until adulthood. However, important variations in the composition and timing of the stages make this conceptualization an oversimplification. Recent work is attempting to accommodate less traditional and nonnuclear family patterns into the family development framework by incorporating divorce, remarriage, single parents, and childlessness into the analysis of life cycle stages (Aldous, 1978; Hill, 1986; Norton, 1983). Changes in the timing of the stages over the life course also need to be considered. For example, in recent decades the period of child rearing has been compressed into fewer years. This change, combined with increased life expectancy, has resulted in a lengthening of the postparental period in the family career.

Stages in the Work Career

The concept of a work career is used by occupational sociologists and organizational psychologists. It has been considered as a two-pronged concept—the external career and the internal career (Bailyn and Schein, 1976; Van Maanen, 1977). The external career can be defined as a "succession of related jobs, arranged in a hierarchy of prestige, through which persons move in an ordered (more-or-less predictable) sequence" (Wilensky, 1961). The internal career focuses on the subjective perception and evaluation of the career by the individual and its role in shaping the individual's identity. Bailyn and Schein (1976) present the following formulation of external career stages that are distinguished according to the tasks to be accomplished:

(I) Preparation—process of choosing and preparing for the career.

(II) Novitiate—period of learning and socialization in which the entrant is assessed in terms of long-range potential.

(III) Early Career—person is fully functioning and doing meaningful though rarely crucial work; further learning and trial.

(IV) Middle Career—person has been fully accepted and is expected to enter period of maximum productivity and performance.

(V) Late Career—person is past the point of maximum productivity though experience allows a high level of contribution and effective teaching of younger people.

(VI) Post Exit—person is no longer officially a member of the occupation but may serve as a consultant or part-time employee.

The length and dynamics of these stages vary by occupation; however, the general pattern holds across occupational categories except for those requiring little skill or training. Variations in the shape of occupational careers are analyzed by looking at the direction and timing of movement over time (Van Maanen, 1977). For example, Gusfield (1961) has mapped out the following shapes: directed careers that follow the general sequence of stages listed; undirected careers in which the individual does not become established or becomes disestablished after a period of establishment; and multiple careers in which the individual goes through the career-establishment process more than once.

The Intersection of Stages in Family and Work Careers

An individual engaged in both a work and family career passes through the stages of both careers simultaneously and is responsible for performing the duties associated with each career at any given time. The analysis of the combined stages of work and family careers is facilitated by conceiving of the intersection as a work/family life cycle. This intersection of stages in work and family careers results in stages of a work/family life cycle that vary in terms of demands, obligations, rewards, and identities.

When changes in patterns of role accumulation are examined over the life course, two modes of coordinating work and family roles emerge as significant, work/family role staging and work/family role allocation. Individuals juggle competing demands by manipulating the timing of activities over stages in the life course. Activities in one domain, either work or family, may be eliminated or postponed until a later stage, thereby creating a more balanced and manageable mix of activities and relationships. This is referred to as work/family role staging.

Individuals also construct and pattern relationships by negotiating and bargaining with significant others in role relationships. Husbands and wives develop patterns of instrumental and expressive interaction by which they evaluate each other's behavior and establish varying degrees of marital cohesion. Marital relations vary systematically according to the extent to which husbands and wives participate in work and family responsibilities (Scanzoni and Scanzoni, 1981). In some families the husband is primarily the economic provider and the wife performs the family work, that is, household duties and childrearing activities. In others both the husband and wife engage in both work and family activities. These varying patterns of work/family role allocation are the product of implicit and explicit negotiation using criteria such as sex-role norms, ability and competence, time and availability, and perceived equity. The allocation of responsibilities between husband and wife can be negotiated several times, resulting in different patterns over the life course.

Both major means of coordinating work and family roles over the life course, work/family role staging and work/family role allocation, may be categorized into two subtypes. Work/family role staging may be either simultaneous or sequential. In simultaneous staging individuals perform both work and family roles across the adult life course. Sequential staging involves shifting the extent of participation in work and family roles across stages in family and work careers, for example, leaving a job to care for small children at home. Work/family role allocation ranges from traditional to symmetrical. In the most traditional pattern the husband is the major breadwinner and the wife performs most of the family work. Symmetrical role allocation involves a relatively interchangeable division of labor in which both husband and wife engage in earning outside the home and family work.

The Traditional-Simultaneous Work/Family Life Cycle

The traditional-simultaneous work/family life cycle consists of the intersection of five stages in the work career and family life cycle:

- Establishment (of family)-Novitiate (in career)
- New Parents-Early Career
- School Age Family-Middle Career
- Postparental Family-Late Career
- Aging Family-Post Exit

This work/family life cycle is characterized by simultaneous participation in work and family roles over the life course. Individuals go through the five stages in each role sequence according to the ideal types outlined in the work and family career literatures. These five stages generally parallel each other in timing. The pattern of role allocation is traditional, that is, the husband is expected to be the major breadwinner with limited responsibilities for family work and the wife is expected to maintain her primary responsibility to the family whether or not she is employed.

Establishment-Novitiate stage. These stages differ in the extent to which they are associated with work/family overload and interference. Interference is high in the Establishment-Novitiate stage. Men are expected to coordinate the timing of marriage and career launching by not marrying until they are able to support a family. The necessity of being able to support a family has its strongest effect on the family formation of those entering occupations with long training periods and those in unstable low-paying jobs. In addition, family responsibilities can hinder career development in the Novitiate stage by limiting training and educational opportunities.

New Parents-Early Career stage. The New Parents-Early Career stage is affected by overload. In the Early Career stage individuals are establishing themselves as full members of their occupations, resulting in a relatively high emphasis on work roles (Hall and Hall, 1979). At the same time young children are very demanding in terms of time, attention, and energy (Aldous, 1978). The high demands of work and family activities among professionals may create unavoidable conflicts at this stage (Edgell, 1970).

School-Age Family-Middle Career stage. Interference is high again in the School-Age Family-Middle Career stage. Timing and scheduling become important as parents are expected to attend school and community functions at times that often conflict with working hours (Harry, 1976). Overload and interference are more likely to derive from parenting activities than from the husband-wife relationship (Pleck, 1979).

Postparental Family-Late Career stage. By the end of the School Age Family-Middle Career stage, established careers require relatively less attention and individuals often have more time for their families. By this stage, however, many husbands and wives have grown apart psychologically and have developed separate interests (Cohen, 1979; Dizard, 1968; Foote, 1963; Steiner, 1972). It is often difficult for couples to reconstruct compatible roles at this point in the family career (Aldous, 1978). Adolescent children often leave home at this time, preventing the development of closer parent-child relationships (Pleck, 1977a). In addition, many middle-aged women seeking to establish careers after their children are grown find themselves responsible for the care of elderly parents (Brody, 1985).

Two-earner families. If both husband and wife pursue a traditional simultaneous work/family life cycle, overload and interference are increased. This pattern is not structurally suited for two-earner families since women often assume major responsibility for family duties and perform tasks that help their husbands advance in their careers. In addition, in the traditional-simultaneous work/family life cycle women maintain these family responsibilities if they become employed. Until recently, most husbands of working wives have spent little, if any, more time in family work than other husbands (Moore and Hofferth, 1979; Pleck and Lang, 1978). Overload and interference among employed women are greatest in the New Parents-Early Career stage (Pleck, 1979). In spite of these limitations many women choose simultaneous participation in work and family activities and relationships with its accompanying stress in order to avoid the greater stress they would feel performing the role of housewife (Bebbington, 1973). Increases in wife employment have provided the major impetus for the construction of alternative work/family life cycles through sequential work/family role staging or symmetrical work/family role allocation.

Sequential staging and symmetrical role allocation are two major ways in which individuals and families attempt to reduce the overload and interference associated with the traditional simultaneous work/family life cycle. Sequential staging is used to alternate the work and family responsibilities of either or both the husband and wife over the life course. Symmetrical role allocation is an attempt to reduce overload and interference by shifting the responsibilities of work and family roles between husband and wife within various stages of the life course.

SEQUENTIAL WORK/FAMILY ROLE STAGING

Sequential staging is the most common type of labor force participation among women (Chenoweth and Maret, 1980). Most sequencing is an adjustment of labor force participation to demands associated with family career stages, especially childbearing. Most married women are employed before their first pregnancy. The employment rate decreases during pregnancy; during the month in which the child is born only one-fifth are still employed. However, by two years after the birth the employment rate has increased to 60% of its previous level. Leaving employment is a more frequent response to the first pregnancy than is a reduction in hours (Waite et al., 1985).

The extent to which employment decreases before the first birth and increases after the birth varies according to the education, prebirth labor force experience, and economic need of the mother. Labor force participation rates are higher before and after the first birth among those with high levels of education and labor force experience. Economic need is not associated with withdrawal from the labor force before the birth but is positively related to returning to work following the birth (McLaughlin, 1982). Among older women, an intermittent work history is associated with family responsibilities, poor health, high family income, migration, and involuntary unemployment (Shaw, 1982).

The following types of sequential work/family participation are most common: (1) conventional, in which a woman quits working when she marries or has children and does not return; (2) early interrupted, in which she stops working for childbearing early in her career development and then returns; (3) late interrupted, in which she establishes her career, quits for a period of childbearing, and then returns; and (4) unstable, in which she alternates between full-time homemaking and paid employment. Sequential staging may be contrasted with simultaneous staging in which women pursue work and family activities across work and family career stages with minimal interruptions for childbearing (Bernard, 1971; Elder, 1977; St. John-Parsons, 1978; Sorensen, 1983). The timing of marriage and parenthood is changing; however, increases in remaining single or childless remain small.

The choice between early and late parenthood is a major element of role staging. This decision involves several trade-offs in the performance of work and family activities over the life course (Wilkie, 1981). Interrupting a work career for early parenthood may increase economic pressures on the family and create some difficulties in reestablishing the career. However, many women find advantages in having children at an age more compatible with others. An early period of childrearing also provides an opportunity for women to formulate future career goals (Daniels and Weingarten, 1982).

Women who postpone the birth of their first child until the Middle Career stage are able to reduce the overload, interference, and economic pressures associated with the New Parent-Early Career stage in the traditional-simultaneous approach. Husband-wife competition in two-career families may be reduced when women are in the career-building stage when their husbands are already established in their work roles. In addition, one partner is relatively more available for performing family responsibilities across several life course stages (Hall and Hall, 1979). It may also be easier to reenter a career after it has been established than to begin one at a later stage in the life course. However, some women find it difficult to interrupt a career once it has been established and others find child rearing to be difficult at a later age.

The following quotes from a study of the timing of parenthood provide examples of some of these trade-offs:

> Motherhood gave me a chance to think about things. I never felt that I was ready after college to move into something earth shattering. I wanted time to think. Having a child around the house is hardly time to think. But it was, actually. As a mother I had a job, and a reason for being. I also had space and time to think about what to do next—a 42-year old job captain in an architectural firm who had her first child at 21 [Daniels and Weingarten, 1982: 95].

> I wanted to be finished with at least something before I became pregnant . . . I didn't want to take time out, or reduce my work

hours, until I was through with my residency. Then I wanted to have my family quickly, because I wanted to get back to work. I planned it quite carefully in my head . . . I would have had a hell of a time if I'd had children earlier. It would have been almost impossible to come where I've come professionally—a 52-year-old psychiatrist who had her first child at 31 [Daniels and Weingarten, 1982: 95, 125].

The increasing numbers of women who are committed to working over the life course find it difficult to engage in extensive work/family role staging. Many of these women perform two full-time jobs—one at work and one at home. This situation prompts a perception that the division of work and family responsibilities is unfair and stimulates calls for the husbands of employed women to do more family work.

SYMMETRICAL WORK/FAMILY
ROLE ALLOCATION

A symmetrical division of labor is the second basic approach for reducing the overload and interference associated with the traditional-simultaneous work/family life cycle. The term "symmetrical family" was used by the English sociologists Michael Young and Peter Willmott (1973) to refer to husband-wife relationships that are "opposite but similar." The term does not imply equality but suggests a move in that direction as compared with traditional families. It suggests less emphasis on sex-based role norms and patterns of differentiation since both husband and wife work outside the home, and both share in the family work. This role differentiation may be accomplished through a process referred to as crossover (Giele, 1980). Crossover is a mechanism by which men and women exchange specialized tasks. Women adopt some traditional male duties such as employment outside the home, and men take on some traditional female family duties. The term does not imply that men and women do the same tasks; it only refers to greater overlap and decreased differentiation based on traditonal sex-role norms.

A major difference between traditional families with some role sharing and symmetrical families with extensive sharing of tasks and responsibilities is one of responsibility. Wives in symmetrical families are co-providers with a responsibility to make a significant economic contribution to the family. In addition, in symmetrical families, husbands move beyond "helping" their wives with family work and assume responsibility in this area. Both responsibilities and task performance are more symmetrical.

The development of symmetrical role allocation has been hindered by the asymmetrical boundaries existing between work and family careers for men and women. Women's work careers have been more vulnerable to family intrusion, whereas men's family careers have been more susceptible to intrusion from work (Pleck, 1977b). Symmetrical role allocation requires more accommodation to family needs by men and more accommodation to work demands by women than the traditional pattern (Bailyn, 1977, 1978; Pleck, 1977b). It also implies a more balanced commitment to both work and family careers by husbands and wives (Rapoport et al., 1974; Scanzoni and Scanzoni, 1981; Young and Willmott, 1973).

Despite the need for this type of role allocation among employed women, progress toward its achievement has been slow. Although husbands of employed women have slightly increased the amount of time they spend in family work in recent years, women still spend considerably more time than men do (Pleck, 1983; Szinovacz, 1984). Many men and some women resist major changes in the direction of symmetrical role allocation (Lein, 1979; Tognoli, 1979). Laura Lein (1979) has examined the ambivalence and resistance to change among traditional husbands. Although these husbands recognize that their employed wives are making an economic contribution to their families, they also see their breadwinner role as their major contribution to their families. This perception is reinforced by their male friends and by some of the wives who have difficulty relinquishing family tasks to their husbands.

Jane Hood's study of couples in which the wife becomes employed reveals examples of this resistance:

> If he [her husband, Martin] ever took a notion to cook, it might be kind of a nuisance. Now when my older son is here, he does cook, and I try to get completely out of the kitchen. If Martin was at all interested in cooking, that's the way I'd have to do it too. . . . It's hard for two people to cook in the kitchen at the same time. . . .

Either this is your meal, or this is my meal. Doing it together does get kind of sticky [Hood, 1983: 101].

I think I do my share. I still feel that she has certain responsibilities to the home. I don't feel for instance, that I should have to cook the meals. But there are a lot of things I'll help her with. When it comes down to whose responsibility it is for some of those things, I feel that it's hers. . . . This equality thing goes only so far. Everybody has to have responsibilities that are theirs [Hood, 1983: 105].

Changes in the structure of work also are necessary to prevent both men and women from being subject to the overload and inter-ference associated with performing two demanding roles with lim-ited flexibility in the work role. When both husband and wife attempt to pursue demanding work over the life course, the development of symmetrical role allocation can reduce overload and interfer-ence for women. However, the total demands on both spouses may still be excessive. In addition, many parents in single-parent families are unable to use role staging and allocation to reduce demands. Overload may best be reduced by permanent part-time employment and job sharing while interference may be dealt with more effectively by flexible work scheduling. These approaches and other changes in the organization of work are discussed in the next chapter.

SUMMARY

This chapter examines the performance of work and family roles in terms of several approaches to multiple roles. Role strain and role expansion theories vary in their predictions regarding the effects of multiple roles on individuals. Empirical research on the effects of women's multiple roles on health and family life indicate that these effects are complex and varied. Studies of women in two-career families illustrate several coping strategies used to deal with role conflict resulting from performing multiple roles.

Individuals coordinate their work and family roles over the life course. This coordination is analyzed by developing the concept of the work/family life cycle and discussing mechanisms of work/family role coordination. Most individuals perform work and family roles that must be coordinated with each other over time. Both work and family roles consist of careers with several stages that vary in their demands, identities, rewards, histories, and projected futures. The stages and associated demands intersect at given points in the life course to form stages in a work/family life cycle. The combined demands from these multiple role activities and relationships may result in work/family overload and interference. Mechanisms used by individuals to construct workable patterns of activities and relationships include work/family role staging and work/family role allocation.

REVIEW QUESTIONS

(1) What is role accumulation?
(2) How can having multiple identities help someone who is performing multiple roles?
(3) Compare and contrast the following types of coping strategies: structural role redefinition, personal role redefinition, and reactive role behaviors.
(4) What does the term *symmetrical family* mean? Under what conditions are symmetrical families likely to occur.
(5) Present and explain the stages in the work/family life cycle.

SUGGESTED PROJECTS

(1) List the work and family roles that you hold. What are some of the activities, identities, rewards, and responsibilites associated with each? How much role strain or conflict do you experience? What would help to ameliorate this conflict?
(2) Consider the portrayal of families on prime-time television. Which programs show symmetrical families and which show traditional families? How are problems of work and family roles generally resolved in these families? How realistic do these patterns of resolution seem to you?

CHAPTER
6

Policy Issues

EARLIER CHAPTERS DOCUMENTED the interdependence of work and family life by examining the worker-earner role of men and women and relationships between several work role characteristics and family life. We also discussed individual means of coordinating work and family demands. This chapter considers how different types of public and private policy address the needs of families deriving from the interdependence of work and family life. Economic policies address problems associated with performing the worker-earner role. The effects of work-role characteristics on family life are altered through family-oriented personnel policies.

ECONOMIC POLICIES

Chapter 2 discussed family responsibility for providing economic resources, the role of the worker-earner role in providing these resources, and problems encountered by families in obtaining adequate resources. This section looks at a range of economic policies that help individuals and families meet their economic needs. These policies are designed to prevent and reduce the major types of economic distress discussed earlier: (1) employment instability and uncertainty and (2) economic deprivation and strain. Major policy areas include full employment, income supports, and occupational segregation and the earnings gap between men and women.

Full Employment

Although the United States government has endorsed full employment as a national goal since 1946, it has no comprehensive policy to ensure employment for all those willing and able to work. Public and private job-creation and job-training programs are instituted at various times, especially during periods of high unemployment. These programs vary in terms of how they attempt to provide employment and in the types of jobs created. Major approaches to the prevention and reduction of employment instability and uncertainty include job creation, job retention, and reemployment.

Job creation. Since 1981 the Reagan administration has approached job creation through policies that promote economic growth. Economic growth in turn is expected to create additional jobs. During the recession of the early 1980s, unemployment levels previously considered unacceptable were perceived by many as the necessary price for economic recovery and lower inflation.

An alternative approach recommends a combination of policies that pursues economic growth while providing jobs for displaced workers through explicit job creation and retention policies. Job creation policies are more effective when they focus on specific types of unemployment, such as unemployment due to recessions, unemployment resulting from structural changes in the economy, and chronic unemployment among those with minimal job qualifications (Buss and Redburn, 1983). The prevention and reduction of one type of unemployment carries over to other types since bumping and skidding processes spread unemployment through the various sectors of the labor force (Ferman and Gardner, 1979). For example, an unemployed skilled worker may take a less skilled job such as car washer or waiter, thereby decreasing job opportunities for unskilled workers. It is also more desirable to create jobs with stability and earning potential rather than low-skilled, dead-end, or temporary jobs.

Job retention. The reduction of employment instability and uncertainty also can be facilitated by job retention strategies such as work sharing and the prevention and regulation of plant closings. Work sharing is an employment policy in which hours worked are reduced instead of having some workers laid off. To prevent work sharing from reducing workers' incomes, unemployment insurance is needed to replace the earnings lost through shorter hours. Work sharing has several advantages to workers: work is distributed more equitably; income reduction is less than during unemployment; and continued employment maintains the individual's provider role and occupational status. However, work-sharing programs tied in with unemployment insurance have encountered some administrative and cost problems (Kerachsky et al., 1986). In addition, work sharing is a form of involuntary part-time employment and not an ideal solution to job shortages.

The prevention and regulation of plant closings can retain jobs and reduce the uncertainty associated with closings. Programs to encourage or subsidize the purchase of marginally profitable plants by employees or others have prevented some closings and served as a viable means of job retention (King, 1982). Preventing plant relocations associated with economic competition and differences in business climate does not necessarily save jobs; however, it can reduce the stress associated with worker relocation and unemployment in communities experiencing closings.

When plant closings cannot be prevented, a notification policy is important to reduce employment uncertainty. A lack of notice creates shock and feelings of helplessness. In the few states with plant-closing legislation, notification requirements vary from a month to a year or more. Based on his study of two plant closings, Sidney Cobb suggested that two or three months' notice is adequate for worker preparation without creating additional stress by extending the process (Slote, 1969). Additional notification is needed, however, if management and workers are to negotiate alternatives to closing, such as employees purchasing the plant.

Reemployment. Job creation and retention policies are broad-based structural approaches to the prevention of economic distress. Other policies and programs reduce the economic distress associated with the unemployment of a major family earner by facilitating reemployment in a comparable position. These policies address three aspects of reemployment: (1) the job search, (2) relocation, and (3) job training. Individuals search for jobs by using state employment services, private placement agencies, direct application, want ads, and informal social networks. Relatively informal means are more effective than placement agencies (Buss and Redburn, 1983; Gordus et al., 1981; Kaufman, 1982). Informal programs such as job clubs frequently provide job-search skills and emotional support in addition to information about available positions.

Some corporations facilitate relocation by providing funds for job seeking and moving or by transferring workers to a facility in a different location. However, relocation assistance has proven to be of limited value. During recessions and periods of high unemployment job shortages preclude successful relocation for most workers. In addition, workers most needing assistance in becoming reemployed, such as older workers with low education and few job skills, tend to resist relocation (Gordus et al., 1981). Last, many workers who do relocate return to their old communities after a short period because they lack the support of family members and friends needed to adjust to a new community (Margolis, 1982).

Job training is designed to facilitate reemployment by upgrading job skills and retraining workers with obsolete skills. However, job training programs generally have low participation rates and unfavorable labor-market outcomes among participants. The lack of participation can be attributed to several factors: inadequate income during training, resistance to changing occupations, anxiety about returning to school, and lack of anticipated benefits among older skilled workers (Buss and Redburn, 1983; Gordus, 1984; Gordus et al., 1981). Under certain conditions job training does not result in satisfactory reemployment, for example, when there are inadequate job opportunities in the new occupation or the new job represents downward mobility. Training programs generally prepare workers for entry-level positions. These positions are more helpful to workers from previously low-paying positions than those displaced from higher-skilled and better-paying jobs. Retraining may be most acceptable to workers who are unwilling to relocate (Kaufman, 1982).

Income Supports

Job creation and retention programs are useful for individuals who are able to work. In many cases, however, individuals are unable to work because of a lack of appropriate skills, disability, family responsibilities, or the unavailability of jobs. Others are unable to earn enough to support a family. Income-support programs are needed to prevent economic deprivation and strain for these individuals and their families. Some programs provide benefits based on previous employment; others are government transfer programs based on economic need.

Unemployment benefits. Unemployment insurance replaces earnings lost during unemployment by providing benefits based on a worker's previous level of earnings and length of employment. However, eligibility requirements prevent many unemployed workers from receiving benefits. Estimates indicate that approximately 45% to 50% of the unemployed receive benefits (Urban League Review, 1976; Margolis, 1982). Other income supplements and protections have even more limited coverage—for example, Sup-

plemental Unemployment Benefits, severance pay, pension vest-
ing, continued health insurance, and home mortgage protection.

   Government transfers. Many workers with the least stable work
histories and fewest job skills are ineligible for work-related unemployment benefits and need assistance from government transfer
programs. In addition, many workers unemployed for long periods
exhaust their unemployment benefits and, after liquidating their
assets, become eligible for government transfer assistance.
   Major government-sponsored transfer programs include Aid to
Families with Dependent Children (AFDC); general welfare assistance; non-cash benefits such as Medicaid, food stamps, and housing subsidies; and Social Security for survivors and the disabled.
The criteria for need and the amount of support provided vary
considerably across programs. In addition, payment levels within
programs may vary from one state to another. For example, in
1982 the average monthly AFDC payments per family ranged
from $573 in the state with the highest payments to $92 in the lowest state (Child Trends, Inc., 1983). As might be expected, these
variations carry over to the extent to which the AFDC program
raises family incomes to or above the poverty level. Before the
Omnibus Budget Reconciliation Act of 1981, a working parent in a
family of three who had earnings equal to the average earnings of
AFDC recipients was able to provide a total disposable income
equal to 101% of the poverty level. This percentage ranged from
67% in Arizona to 130% in Vermont. In 1982 the same level of
earnings combined with the reduced AFDC payments provided an
average income that was 81% of the poverty level. The state-level
percentages ranged from 62% in Alabama and Georgia to 96% in
Rhode Island (U.S. Commission on Civil Rights, 1983).
   These government programs are not integrated into a comprehensive policy that provides a minimum income for American families. Both employment-based and government transfer programs
are inadequate to meet the needs of the unemployed and the poor.
These programs form a patchwork system of support associated
with inequities derived from variations in eligibility for, amount of,
and duration of benefits; varied levels of stigma; loss of status and
damage to the provider role; and limited and varied reductions of
economic deprivation and strain. For example, men are more likely
to be eligible for unemployment insurance, whereas women are

more often dependent on programs such as AFDC for support. Since unemployment insurance is based on previous employment experience, it is associated with less stigma than government transfer programs such as AFDC.

Many women who become heads of families due to death, divorce, or illegitimacy are ill-prepared for self-support. Time is required for educational preparation and training. This transition is a major component of temporary poverty, which if not handled adequately becomes persistent poverty. Some type of family allowance could provide opportunities for women to care for their young children and participate in educational and job-training programs. Women with or without husbands must recognize the risks involved in not preparing for paid work even if they intend to be full-time homemakers. Current welfare programs do not create opportunities for recipients to get the training and experience needed to move out of poverty.

A comprehensive employment and income policy is needed to reduce employment instability and economic strain among families. A policy of full employment needs to be combined with a comprehensive income-support program for those unable to work and those unable to provide adequate incomes to their families. Since studies have shown that income-support programs do not significantly limit the incentive to work (Kelly, 1985), the two approaches complement each other in preventing economic distress.

Occupational Segregation and the Earnings Gap

In Chapter 2 we discussed occupational segregation and the earnings gap between men and women. Policies to address this situation involve hiring and comparable worth programs for occupations held mainly by men and women.

Hiring policies. Title VII of the Civil Rights Act of 1964 and other equal employment legislation make it unlawful to discriminate in hiring, training, promotions, and salaries because of sex, race, or national origin. Federal agencies such as the Equal Employment Opportunity Commission have been established to enforce this legislation. Over the past 20 years some progress has been made in reducing occupational segregation. More women and minorities are employed in still predominantly male occupations such as high-level professional and managerial positions, carpenter, machinist, telephone installer and repairer, police officer, fire fighter, and construction worker. However, challenges to the enforcement of government regulations and affirmative action programs continue; for example, recent court cases are attempting to remove hiring quotas for women and minorities.

Comparable worth. It is frequently recommended that women and minorities locked into low-paying jobs with few opportunities for advancement be assisted in obtaining higher-paying predominantly male jobs. The redistribution of women and minorities into higher-paying jobs with opportunities for advancement would obviously benefit those who are successful. In addition, higher numbers of women and minorities in policymaking positions could influence employment policy to the advantage of those still in the secondary labor market. However, more is needed. Many of the low-paying dead-end jobs that women would leave for more lucrative positons are jobs that support women's traditional caring functions, for example, child care, nursing home care, and other services to those in need. If the number and quality of these services decrease, many women would be unable to maintain and progress in these new jobs because of their traditional responsibilities for dependents. Therefore, the elimination of the sources of the feminization of poverty depends not only on the movement of women into primary-sector jobs but also on upgrading jobs that women depend upon in order to participate fully in new opportunities.

One proposed solution to women's lower wages is the initiation of comparable worth programs. The Equal Pay Act of 1963 requires equal pay for equal work, that is, work "which requires equal skill, effort, and responsibility . . . performed under similar working conditions" (U.S. Commission on Civil Rights, 1983: 25). Comparable worth, on the other hand, is based on the idea that "within a given organization, jobs that are equal in their value to the organization ought to be eqully compensated, whether or not the work content of these jobs is similar" (U.S. Commission on Civil Rights, 1983: 25).

Studies indicate that women's jobs often are paid less on average than men's jobs with similar scores derived from job evaluation plans. These evaluation plans typically give points for basic features of jobs such as skills, effort, responsibility, and working conditions. For example, in Washington state licensed practical nurses, typically female, and correctional officers, predominantly male, receive the same score on a job evaluation; however, correctional officers earn $406 more per month than nurses. In San Jose, California, senior librarians earn $221 less per month than senior chemists despite their equal scores on a job evaluation (U.S. Commission on Civil Rights, 1983).

This approach to pay equity remains controversial. Some argue that job evaluation programs are inadequate tools for determining comparable worth when job tasks are dissimilar; others argue that wage rates are properly determined by the supply and demand of various workers in the labor force. However, the degree of association between wage levels and the predominance of males and females in given occupations suggest systematic differences in wage levels by sex.

In recent years, comparable worth cases have begun to appear in court; decisions in these cases have yielded mixed results. In 1985 the state of Washington adopted a comparable worth policy despite the fact that a court decision favoring comparable worth was overruled by a higher court. This approach is gaining momentum as a means to reduce further sex discrimination in employment. The extent to which it is effective will be determined over the next several years.

FAMILY-ORIENTED PERSONNEL POLICIES

Increasing recognition of the impact of work-role characteristics on the quality of family life and employee attitudes and productivity has led to initiatives in the development of family-oriented personnel policies. Family-oriented personnel policies address the effects of work-role characteristics on family life discussed in Chapter 4. These characteristics include amount and scheduling of work time, work-related geographic mobility, and psychological and physical demands associated with work. This section describes several types of family-oriented personnel policies including alternate work schedules, parental leaves, child care, flexible benefit

plans, counseling and education programs, and relocation policies. First, we will provide an overview of family-oriented personnel policies from the perspectives of families and corporations.

Family Perspectives

Recent information documents the needs of working parents for
family-oriented personnel policies as perceived by parents and
others interested in the well-being of families. For example, the
highest-ranking policy recommendation from the 1980 White
House Conference on Families called for family-oriented personnel policies including flextime, shared and part-time jobs with benefits, leave policies, transfer policies, and child care (White House
Conference on Families, 1980). In addition, in the national survey conducted by Louis Harris and Associates for the General Mills
American Family Report (Harris and associates, 1981), family
members, especially working mothers, indicate several employment policies and benefit plans that would help them balance their
family and work responsibilities. Those reported to be most helpful
include the freedom to choose the benefits that best suit their needs
(flexible benefit plans) and several types of flexible work schedules. Leave days especially designated for child care and child-care
facilities at the workplace were less frequently perceived as helpful.

These data suggest that working parents prefer employment policies providing the flexibility to meet specific needs without being
targeted to those needs. This approach is well suited to changing
family needs over the work/family life cycle. For example, the
benefit needs of parents of young children differ from those of parents with grown children preparing for retirement. To be more specific, families with preschool children need one type of child care;
those with school-aged children need a different type.

Corporate Perspectives

As the numbers of women workers and men who are members
of dual-career families have increased, corporations have found it
necessary to adjust their personnel policies to address the needs of
these workers. These policy changes are designed to recruit and
retain productive workers. For example, family-oriented personnel

policies such as flexible work schedules and child care are relatively extensive among hospitals employing large numbers of nurses, an occupation currently in high demand.

Recent research suggests room for additional policy initiatives by corporations. A survey conducted by Catalyst in 1980 (Catalyst, 1981) including responses from 374 of the top 1300 *Fortune* corporations indicates a large gap between the percentage favoring family-oriented personnel practices and the percentage enacting these policies. For example:

	Have	Favor
Flexible work hours	37%	73%
Flexible benefit plans	8%	62%
Monetary support for child care	19%	54%

Three-fourths of the corporate representatives reported concern with two-career family issues because of possible impacts on recruitment, employee morale, productivity, and profits. A majority of human resource executives interviewed in the Louis Harris-General Mills Survey expected their organizations to adopt the following policies and benefits within the next five years: child care at the workplace, flexible benefit plans, job sharing, and several types of flexible work schedules (Harris and associates, 1981).

In addition to corporations, the military services have developed extensive programs to meet the needs of families. Until recently, military policies assumed that the bulk of members of the military, especially nonofficers, were unmarried. During the past decade, the number of married members of the military increased dramatically. With this shift the rate of retention dropped. In response, all branches of the military have developed family-oriented programs including family support centers, programs dealing with issues such as family violence and money management, child-care programs, and programs to reduce or ease the problems associated with separation and frequent relocation.

Alternate Work Schedules

Work schedules other than working from 9 to 5 five days a week are among the most frequently established family-oriented personnel policies. These alternate work schedules include flextime and part-time work, which were discussed in Chapter 4. Their popularity derives from their fit with corporate needs. For example, flextime was originally developed to reduce commuting time, conserve energy, use expensive equipment more efficiently, and keep businesses open longer hours to meet customer needs. Many retail establishments and banks need part-time workers because of peak business periods during the day. They are referred to as family-oriented policies because they are often used by workers to facilitate work/family role coordination. Workers on flextime schedules are better able to be at home when their children are home and many women prefer part-time work to prevent and reduce overload. Part-time work, however, is often associated with a lack of benefits and opportunities for advancement.

Parental Leaves

Policy issues surrounding parental leaves focus on two components: medical leave for pregnancy and childbirth and child-care leave. Medical leave associated with pregnancy and childbirth generally consists of no more than six weeks of disability pay (Axel, 1985). The legal basis for maternity leave is rooted in laws regarding sex discimination in employment. The Pregnancy Discrimination Act of 1978 requires that companies providing health insurance or disability leaves for other medical conditions must cover pregnancy and childbirth as a medical disability.

Until recently, parental leaves have consisted almost entirely of medical maternity leaves. Additional unpaid personal leave to care for a newborn child is now available in many large corporations. The total leave period generally does not exceed three months. If the woman returns within the eligible leave time, a job at a comparable level is usually guaranteed by the employer (Axel, 1985).

In recent years, attempts have been made to include men in programs providing personal leave for newborn care. At this writing only a handful of programs provide paid or unpaid parental leaves for fathers (Pleck, 1986). In the spring of 1986, the Parental and Medical Leave Act was introduced in the U.S. Congress. This bill would require employers to provide a minumum of 18 weeks unpaid job-protected leave for any mother or father choosing to stay home to care for newborn, adopted, or seriously ill children. Some argue that parental leaves for both mothers and fathers have been discouraged by the acceptance of the principle that pregnancy is a female medical disability. Viewing childbirth as a larger process including newborn care could expand support for parental leave for both mothers and fathers. This approach also has been taken by advocates of parental leave for adoptive parents.

Child Care

Although child-care facilities at the workplace are not seen as especially helpful to working parents in the Harris Survey, the need for child care of some type is critical. Whether parents prefer child care at the workplace or would rather have the flexibility to make other arrangements, working parents must provide care for each child for several years. Lack of adequate child care prevents parents, especially mothers, from being able to take needed jobs, restricts them to part-time jobs that are traditionally low paying and lacking in opportunities for advancement, and prevents them from seeking promotions and jobs requiring high levels of involvement (U.S. Commission on Civil Rights, 1981).

The number of children in different types of child-care arrangements at any one time is difficult to determine. However, it is clear that parents use a wide range of types of child care and many use more than one type at a time. More than 70% of children aged three to five with employed mothers are in some form of group child-care program, for example, nursery school or kindergarten. Approximately one-third were enrolled in full-day programs in 1980. In 1977 about 42% of three- and four-year-old children of full-time working mothers were cared for in someone else's home, usually a family day-care home in which an adult cares for several children. These figures indicate the overlap among types of care. Many women work longer hours than are provided in preschool programs such as nursery schools. Children under three are most likely to be cared for in family day-care homes. In 1977 approximately one-third of children under three whose mothers worked full-time were cared for in this way. Some families make other arrangements such as having mothers and fathers work different hours so that one parent is home to care for children at all times (Kamerman, 1983).

Many corporations are considering some type of support for the care of their employees' children as a means of recruiting and retaining desirable employees and of reducing absenteeism and turnover. The extent and type of support is dependent on tax incentives provided for employers who support child-care programs. Child-care facilities at the workplace are only one way, and generally one of the least feasible approaches, in which corporations increase child-care resources for working parents. Other ways in which corporations become involved in child-care issues include providing support to the following types of programs: existing child-care programs, information and referral systems, family day-care programs, "sick child" care programs, after-school programs, vouchers for parents to use for child care, the inclusion of child care in flexible benefit plans, and the purchase of slots in existing centers for employee use. In addition, some recognize the need to extend child-care policies to cover dependent care that includes care for ill, disabled, and elderly family members as well as young children.

Flexible Benefit Plans

Employee benefits are a major component of an individual's total compensation for working. A recent survey estimates that benefits average an additional 37% of wages and salaries (Axel, 1985). Thus benefits have important implications for both employers and employees. Traditional benefits include social security taxes, contributions to unemployment insurance, life and health insurance premiums, private pensions, and pay for vacations, holidays, and sick leave. Flexible benefit plans allow employees to select among benefits according to their needs. For example, in two-earner couples where both are covered by health insurance, one partner can omit health insurance in return for more vacation time or life insurance.

This approach helps families and working parents because of the variety of family structures and the changes in family-related employment problems over the work/family life cycle. Flexible benefit plans assist corporations in containing costs and providing equity among employees in different family situations. Following tax legislation in 1978 that provided certain tax allowances, several major corporations initiated flexible benefit plans. However, during 1984 regulations from the Internal Revenue Service, the Treasury Department, and Congress reversed some of the allowances provided in 1978 (Karp, 1985). The 1984 regulations were maintained in the recent tax reform act.

Counseling and Education

Counseling and education programs have increased in frequency and popularity in recent years. These programs address several work/family issues such as parenting, coordinating work and family responsibilities, job stress, and money management skills. Much employee counseling takes place under the auspices of Employee Assistance Programs (EAPs). Originally EAPs were designed as alcohol and drug abuse programs. In recent years they have expanded to deal with other types of problems such as marital/family discord, job-related stress, legal or financial difficulties, and emotional or social concerns. Employers are concerned about these problems because they are manifested in the workplace through excessive tardiness, high rates of absenteeism, low quality and quantity of work, higher sickness and accident insurance claims, and higher health benefits utilization.

Programs with an educational focus also address work/family issues. Private consulting firms and organizations such as state departments of vocational and career education have developed programs that are offered to employee groups, usually through corporate personnel departments. These programs deal with issues such as parenting in single-parent and two-earner families, child development, managing time and energy, balancing work and family life, the division of family responsibilities, strengthening family life, and health and fitness. They are usually held at the workplace during lunch or after regular working hours. These programs are a relatively inexpensive way for employers to facilitate work/family role coordination among their employees.

Relocation

In Chapter 4 we discussed the significance of job transfers and relocation for employers, employees, and families. Until recently corporate relocation packages for managerial and professional employees included benefits such as purchasing the employee's former home, shipping household goods, and providing a temporary living allowance during the move. As the costs of moving increased over the past decade, some corporations added other monetary benefits including a mortgage interest differential allowance, direct mortgage assistance, cost of living allowances, term loans, and salary increases (Moore, 1981). Some employers also provide information about schools, transportation, and housing in the new community. As two-career families became more prevalent, corporations began to assist spouses in finding jobs in the new community through resumé preparation and arranging job interviews. In addition, some companies are becoming more flexible in their transfer policies by providing employees with more choices regarding the number, timing, and location of transfers.

Implications for Men and Women

These policies have the potential of facilitating work/family role coordination among men and women over the work/family life cycle. However, it is not enough to change the structure of jobs and provide programs and policies to facilitate work/family integration if the norms and expectations associated with them mediate against their use by both men and women. As Pleck (1986) has pointed out, the removal of institutional barriers through family-oriented personnel policies should not be expected to increase family role participation among fathers in the absence of motivation, skills, and supports. Since many family-oriented personnel policies are considered appropriate for women but not for men, it is not surprising that men do not use them in large numbers.

Implicit career penalties also are associated with the use of some family-oriented personnel policies. For example, employees sometimes are informed that there is no penalty for refusing job transfers. However, if an employee refuses more transfers than is informally acceptable in that company, he or she is considered not sufficiently committed to the job and is passed over for promotions.

If the use of policies that facilitate work/family integration are considered appropriate only for women or are accompanied by career penalties, men and women wanting both career advancement and children will continue to face difficult problems. Janet and Larry Hunt (1977) have suggested that two classes of workers may emerge, work-oriented nonparents and family-oriented parents. This situation would impose unpleasant choices on individual families and create economic difficulties among families with children.

Providing family-oriented personnel policies for men and women would benefit both family life and the workplace. Women and families would no longer suffer career penalties and men would have more options for combining their work and family roles. In addition, the productivity of a broader segment of the population would be available to the labor force and the economy.

SUMMARY

These policies address the two major components involved in the coordination of work and family roles. Economic policies address problems associated with performing the worker-earner role including unemployment, inadequate incomes, and discrimination in hiring and wages. Family-oriented personnel policies are developed by employers to attract and retain employees and to reduce absenteeism, turnover, and low productivity. These policies address employer concerns because they enable individuals and families to reduce the work/family overload and interference associated with work-role characteristics and the demands of family life. Family-oriented personnel policies benefiting workers, families, and employers include alternate work schedules, parental leaves, child care, flexible benefit plans, counseling and education programs, and relocation policies.

REVIEW QUESTIONS

(1) What are some of the public policies that might reduce employment instability and uncertainty?
(2) Explain why income-support programs are often necessary for people experiencing unemployment.
(3) What does occupational segregation mean?

(4) Describe some policies that are aimed at addressing the earnings gap between men and women.
(5) List some of the personnel policies that would directly affect the well-being of families.

SUGGESTED PROJECTS

(1) Suppose that you were just elected to the U.S. Senate. What governmental policies would you pursue to strengthen families in this country? What arguments would you use to support them? What kinds of criticisms would you expect to hear from your colleagues and constituencies?
(2) Interview someone employed by a large corporation regarding its personnel policies. To what extent do these policies meet the needs of two-earner families?

References

ALDOUS, J. (1978) Family Careers: Developmental Change in Families. New York: John Wiley.

ALDOUS, J., M. OSMOND, and M. HICKS (1979) "Men's work and men's families," pp. 227-256 in W. Burr et al. (eds.) Contemporary Theories about the Family, vol. 1. New York: Free Press.

ANDERSON, R. N. (1980) "Rural plant closures: the coping behavior of Filipinos in Hawaii." Family Relations 29: 511-516.

ANESHENSEL, C. S. (1986) "Marital and employment role-strain, social support, and depression among adult women," in S. E. Hobfoll (ed.) Stress, Social Support, and Women. Washington, DC: Hemisphere.

ANESHENSEL, C., R. R. FRERICHS, and V. A. CLARK (1982) "Family roles and sex differences in depression." Journal of Health and Social Behavior 22: 379-393.

ANGELL, R. C. (1936) The Family Encounters the Depression. New York: Scribner.

AXEL, H. (1985) Corporations and Families: Changing Practices and Perspectives. New York: Conference Board.

BAILYN, L. (1970) "Career and family orientations of husbands and wives in relation to marital happiness." Human Relations 23: 97-113.

BAILYN, L. (1977) "Involvement and accommodation in technical careers," pp. 109-132 in J. Van Maanen (ed.) Organizational Careers. New York: John Wiley.

BAILYN, L. (1978) "Accommodation of work to family," pp. 159-174 in R. Rapoport and R. Rapoport (eds.) Working Couples. New York: Harper & Row.

BAILYN, L. and E. SCHEIN (1976) "Life/career considerations as indicators of quality of employment," pp. 151-163 in A. D. Biderman and T. F. Drury (eds.) Measuring Work Quality for Social Reporting. Beverly Hills, CA: Sage.

BAKKE, E. W. (1940) Citizens Without Work. New Haven: Yale University Press.

BARRETT, N. S. (1979a) "Women in the job market: occupations, earnings, and career opportunities," pp. 31-61 in R. E. Smith (ed.) The Subtle Revolution. Washington, DC: Urban Institute.

BARRETT, N. S. (1979b) "Women in the job market: unemployment and work schedules," in R. E. Smith (ed.) The Subtle Revolution. Washington, DC: Urban Institute.

BARTLETT, R. L. and C. CALLAHAN, III (1984) "Wage determination and marital status: another look." Industrial Relations 23: 90-96.

BEBBINGTON, A. C. (1973) "The function of stress in the establishment of the dual-career family." Journal of Marriage and the Family 35: 530-537.

BERNARD, J. (1971) Women and the Public Interest. Chicago: Aldine, Atherton.

BEST, F. (1980) Flexible Life Scheduling. New York: Praeger.

BEUTELL, N. J. and J. H. GREENHAUS (1983) "Integration of home and non-home roles: women's conflict and coping behavior." Journal of Applied Psychology 68: 43-48.

BLAKELY, E. J. and P. P. SHAPIRA (1984) "Industrial restructuring and policies for public investment in advanced industrial societies." Annals of the American Academy of Political and Social Science 475: 96-109.

BLECHMAN, E. A. (1982) "Are children with one parent at psychological risk?" Journal of Marriage and the Family 44: 179-195.

BOHEN, H. and A. VIVEROS-LONG (1981) Balancing Jobs and Family Life. Philadelphia: Temple University Press.

BOSS, P. G., H. I. McCUBBIN, and G. LESTER (1979) "The corporate executive wife's coping patterns in response to routine husband/father absence." Family Process 18: 79-86.

BOULD, S. (1977) "Female-headed families: personal fate control and the provider role." Journal of Marriage and the Family 39: 339-349.

BRETT, J. M. (1982) "Job transfer and well-being." Journal of Applied Psychology 67: 450-463.

BRETT, J. M. and J. D. WERBEL (1980) "The effect of job transfer on employees and their families." Washington, DC: Employee Relocation Council.

BRODY, E. (1985) "Parent care as a normative family stress." Gerontologist 25: 19-29.

BRONFENBRENNER, U. and A. C. CROUTER (1982) "Work and family through time and space," pp. 39-83 in S. B. Kamerman and S. D. Hayes (eds.) Families That Work. Washington, DC: National Academy Press.

BURDEN, D. S. (1986) "Single parents and the work setting: the impact of multiple job/homelife responsibilities." Family Relations 35: 37-43.

BURKE, R. J. and T. WEIR (1975) "The husband-wife relationship." Business Quarterly 40: 62-67.

BURKE, R. J. and T. WEIR (1977) "Marital helping relationships." Journal of Psychology 95: 121-130.

BURKE, R. J., T. WEIR, and R. F. DuWORS, Jr. (1980) "Work demands on administrators and spouse well-being." Human Relations 33: 253-278.

BURR, W. R., G. K. LEIGH, R. D. DAY, and J. CONSTANTINE (1979) "Symbolic interaction and the family," pp. 42-111 in W.R. Burr et al. (eds.) Contemporary Theories about the Family, vol. II. New York: Free Press.

BUSS, T. F., and F. S. REDBURN (1983) Shutdown at Youngstown. Albany: State University of New York Press.

BUSS, T. F. and F. S. REDBURN with J. WALDRUN (1983) Mass Unemployment: Plant Closings and Community Mental Health. Beverly Hills, CA: Sage.

Catalyst (1981) Corporations and Two-Career Families. New York: Author.

CAVAN, R. S. and K. H. RANCK (1938) The Family and the Depression. Chicago: University of Chicago Press.

CAZENAVE, N. A. (1979) "Middle-income black fathers: an analysis of the provider role." Family Coordinator 28: 583-593.

CHENOWETH, L. and E. MARET (1980) "The career patterns of mature American women." Sociology of Work and Occupations 7: 222-251.

CHERLIN, A. (1979) "Work life and marital dissolution," in G. Levinger and O. C. Moles (eds.) Divorce and Separation: Context, Causes, and Consequences. New York: Basic Books.

Child Trends, Inc. (1983) U.S. Children and Their Families. Washington: Government Printing Office.

CLEARY, P. and D. MECHANIC (1983) "Sex differences in psychological distress among married people." Journal of Health and Social Behavior 24: 111-121.

COBB, S. and S. KASL (1977) Termination. Cincinnati, OH: National Institute of Occupational Safety and Health.

COHEN, J. (1979) "Male roles in mid-life." Family Coordinator 28: 465-471.

COHN, R. M. (1978) "The effect of employment status change on self-attitudes." Social Psychology 41: 81-93.

COOKE, R. A. and D. M. ROUSSEAU (1984) "Stress and strain from family roles and work-role expectations." Journal of Applied Psychology 69: 252-260.

COSER, R. L. (1985) "Power lost and status gained: the American middle-class husband." Presented at the Annual Meeting of the American Sociological Association, Washington, DC.

COSTELLO, J. (1976) "Why more managers are refusing transfers." Nation's Business (October): 4-5.

CRAMER, J. C. (1980) "Fertility and female employment: problems of causal direction." American Sociological Review 45: 167-190.

DANIELS, P. and K. WEINGARTEN (1982) Sooner or Later: The Timing of Parenthood in Adult Lives. New York: W.W. Norton.

DEMPSTER-McCLAIN, D. I. and P. MOEN (1983) "Work-time involvement and preferences of employed parents." Presented at the Annual Meeting of the National Council on Family Relations, St. Paul, MN.

DEVALL, E., Z. STONEMAN, and G. BRODY (1986) "The impact of divorce and maternal employment on pre-adolescent children." Family Relations 35: 153-159.

DEVENS, R. M., Jr., C. B. LEON, and D. L. SPRINKLE (1985) "Employment and unemployment in 1984: a second year of strong growth in jobs." Monthly Labor Review (February): 3-15.

DIZARD, J. (1968) Social Change in the Family. Chicago: University of Chicago.

DUNCAN, G. J. (1984) Years of Poverty, Years of Plenty. Ann Arbor, MI: Institute for Social Research.

DUNCAN, G. J. and S. D. HOFFMAN (1985) "A reconsideration of the economic consequences of marital dissolution." Demography 22: 485-497.

DUNCAN, R. P. and C. PERRUCCI (1976) "Dual occupation families and migration." American Sociological Review 41: 252-261.

EDGELL, S. (1970) "Spiralists: their careers and family lives." British Journal of Sociology 21: 314-323.

ELDER, G. H., Jr. (1974) Children of the Great Depression. Chicago: University of Chicago.

ELDER, G. H., Jr. (1977) "Family history and the life course." Journal of Family History 2: 279-304.

ELDER, G. H., Jr., T. VAN NGUYEN, and A. CASPI (1985) "Linking family hardship to children's lives." Child Development 56: 361-375.

ELMAN, M. R. and L. A. GILBERT (1984) "Coping strategies for role conflict in married professional women with children." Family Relations 33: 317-327.

ESTES, R. J. and H. L. WILENSKY (1978) "Life cycle squeeze and the morale curve." Social Problems 25: 227-292.

FARRAN, D. C. and L. H. MARGOLIS (1983) "The impact of paternal job loss on the family." Presented at the Annual Meeting of the Society for Research in Child Development, Detroit.

FELDBERG, R. L. and E. GLENN (1979) "Male and female: job versus gender models in the sociology of work." Social Problems 26: 524-538.

FELMLEE, D. H. (1984) "A dynamic analysis of women's employment exits." Demography 21: 171-183.

FERMAN, L. A. and J. GARDNER (1979) "Economic deprivation, social mobility, and mental health," pp. 193-224 in L. A. Ferman and J. P. Gordus (eds.) Mental Health and the Economy. Kalamazoo, MI: Upjohn Institute.

FIGUERIA-McDONALD, J. (1978) "Mental health among unemployed Detroiters." Social Service Review 52: 383-399.

FINCH, J. (1983) Married to the Job: Wive's Incorporation in Men's Work. London: Allen & Unwin.

FINN, P. (1981) "The effects of shift work on the lives of employees." Monthly Labor Review: 31-34.

FLAIM, P. O. and E. SEHGAL (1985) "Displaced workers of 1979-83: how well have they fared?" Monthly Labor Review (June): 3-16.

FOOTE, N. N. (1963) "Matching of husband and wife in phases of development," pp. 15-21 in M. B. Sussman (ed.) Sourcebook in Marriage and the Family. Boston: Houghton Mifflin.

FOSTER, M. A., B. S. WALLSTON, and M. BERGER (1980) "Feminist orientation and job-seeking behavior among dual-career couples." Sex Roles 6: 59-65.

FOX, G. L., R. F. KELLY, and A. W. SHELDON (1982) "Family responses to economic distress in the Detroit metropolitan area." Presented at the Annual Meetings of the North Central Sociological Association, Detroit.

FOX, M. F. and S. HESSE-BIBER (1983) American Women at Work. Palo Alto, CA: Mayfield Publishing Company.

FURSTENBERG, F. (1974) "Work experience and family life," in J. O'Toole (ed.) Work and the Quality of Life. Cambridge, MA: MIT Press.

GAYLORD, M. (1979) "Relocation and the corporate family: unexplored issues." Social Work (May): 186-191.

GERSTEL, N. and H. GROSS (1984) Commuter Marriage. New York: Guilford.

GIELE, J. Z. (1980) "Crossovers: new themes in adult roles and the life cycle," pp. 3-15 in D. G. McGuigan (ed.) Women's Lives. Ann Arbor: University of Michigan.

GONGLA, P. A. (1982) "Single parent families: a look at families of mothers and children." Marriage and Family Review 5: 5-27.

GOODE, W. J. (1960) "A theory of role strain." American Sociological Review 25: 483-496.

GORDUS, J. P. (1984) "The human resource implications of plant shutdowns." Annals of the American Academy of Political and Social Science 475: 66-79.

GORDUS, J. P., P. JARLEY, and L. A. FERMAN (1981) Plant Closings and Economic Dislocation. Kalamazoo, MI: Upjohn Institute.

GORE, S. (1977) "Social supports and unemployment stress." Presented at the Annual Meeting of the American Sociological Association.

GORE, S. and T. W. MANGIONE (1983) "Social roles, sex roles and psychological distress." Journal of Health and Social Behavior 24: 300-312.

GOULD, S. and J. D. WERBEL (1983) "Work involvement: a comparison of dual wage earner and single wage earner families." Journal of Applied Psychology 68: 313-319.

GOVE, W. R. and M. R. GEERKEN (1977) "The effect of children and employ-
    ment on the mental health of married men and women." Social Forces 56:
    66-85.
GREENHAUS, J. H. and R. E. KOPELMAN (1981) "Conflict between work and
    nonwork roles: implications for the career planning process." Human
    Resource Planning 4: 1-10.
GRIMM, J. W. and R. N. STERN (1974) "Sex roles and internal labor market
    structures: the 'female' semi-professions." Social Problems 21: 690-705.
GROAT, H. T., R. L. WORKMAN, and A. G. NEAL (1976) "Labor force partici-
    pation and family formation." Demography 13: 115-125.
GROSSMAN, A. S. (1982) "More than half of all children have working moth-
    ers." Monthly Labor Review 195: 41-43.
GUSFIELD, J. (1961) "Occupational roles and forms of enterprise." American
    Journal of Sociology 66: 571-580.
HALL, D. T. (1972) "A model of coping with role conflict." Administrative Sci-
    ence Quarterly 4: 471-486.
HALL, F. S. and D. T. HALL (1979) The Two-Career Couple. Reading, MA:
    Addison-Wesley.
HANSON, S. L. (1983) "A family life-cycle approach to the socioeconomic
    attainment of working women." Journal of Marriage and the Family 45: 323-
    338.
HAREVEN, T. (1977) Family and Kin in Urban Communities, 1700-1930. New
    York: New Viewpoints.
HARRIS, L. (1982) "Recession: direct hit on 1 family in 3." Detroit Free Press
    (December 9): 12A.
HARRIS, L. and Associates, Inc. (1981) Families at Work. Minneapolis, MN:
    General Mills, Inc.
HARRISON, A. and J. MINOR (1978) "Interrole conflict, coping strategies and
    satisfaction among black working wives." Journal of Marriage and the Family
    40: 799-805.
HARRY, J. (1976) "Evolving sources of happiness for men over the life cycle: a
    structural analysis." Journal of Marriage and the Family 38: 289-296.
HAYGHE, H. (1981) "Husbands and wives as earners: an analysis of family
    data." Monthly Labor Review (February): 46-52.
HAYGHE, H. (1982) "Dual-earner families: their economic and demographic
    characteristics," pp. 27-40 in J. Aldous (ed.) Two Paychecks: Life in Dual-
    Earner Families. Beverly Hills, CA: Sage.
HAYGHE, H. (1984) "Working mothers reach record number in 1984." Monthly
    Labor Review (December): 31-34.
HAYGHE, H. (1986) "Rise in mothers' labor force activity includes those with
    infants." Monthly Labor Review (February): 43-45.
HAYNES, S. G. and M. FEINLEIB (1980) "Women, work and coronary heart
    disease." American Journal of Public Health 70: 133-141.
HEDGES, J. and E. SEKSCENSKI (1979) "Workers on late shifts in a changing
    economy." Monthly Labor Review 102 (September): 14-22.
HEDGES, J. N. and D. E. TAYLOR (1980) "Recent trends in worktime: hours
    edge downward." Monthly Labor Review (March): 3-11.

HILL, M. S. (1979) "The wage effects of marital status and children." Journal of Human Resources 14: 579-593.

HILL, R. (1964) "Methodological issues in family development research." Family Process 3: 186-206.

HILL, R. (1986) "Life cycle stages for types of single parent families." Family Relations 35: 19-29.

HILLER, D. V. and W. W. PHILLIBER (1986) "The division of labor in contemporary marriage: expectations, perceptions, and performance." Social Problems 33: 191-201.

HOFFERTH, S. L. (1984) "Long-term economic consequences for women of delayed childbearing and reduced family size." Demography 42: 141-155.

HOFFERTH, S. L. and K. A. MOORE (1979) "Early childbearing and later economic well-being." American Sociological Review 44: 784-815.

HOFFMAN, L. W. (1979) "Maternal employment: 1979." American Psychologist 34: 859-865.

HOOD, J. C. (1983) Becoming a Two-Job Family. New York: Praeger.

HOOD, J. C. (1986) "The provider role: Its meaning and measurement." Journal of Marriage and the Family 48 (May): 349-359.

HOOD, J. C. and S. GOLDEN (1979) "Beating time/making time." Family Coordinator 28: 575-582.

HORNUNG, C. A. and B. C. McCULLOUGH (1981) "Status relationships in dual-employment marriages: consequences for psychological well-being." Journal of Marriage and the Family 43: 125-141.

HORNUNG, C. A., B. C. McCULLOUGH, and T. SUGIMOTO (1981) "Status relationships in marriage: risk factors in spouse abuse." Journal of Marriage and the Family 43: 675-692.

HUDIS, P. M. (1976) "Commitment to work and to family: marital status differences in women's earning." Journal of Marriage and the Family 38: 267-278.

HUNT, J. G. and L. L. HUNT (1977) "Dilemmas and contradictions of status." Social Problems 24: 407-416.

JAHODA, M. (1982) Employment and Unemployment. New York: Cambridge University Press.

JOHNSON, B. L. (1980) "Marital and family characteristics of the labor force, March 1979." Monthly Labor Review (April): 48-52.

JOHNSON, B. L. and E. WALDMAN (1981) "Marital and family patterns of the labor force." Monthly Labor Review 104: 36-38.

JOHNSON, B. L. and E. WALDMAN (1983) "Most women who maintain families receive poor labor market returns." Monthly Labor Review (December): 30-34.

JONES, A. P. and M. C. BUTLER (1980) "A role transition approach to the stress of organizationally induced family role disruption." Journal of Marriage and the Family 42: 367-376.

JONES, S. B. (1973) "Geographic mobility as seen by the wife and mother." Journal of Marriage and the Family 35: 210-218.

KAMERMAN, S. B. (1983) "Child-care services: a national perspective." Monthly Labor Review (December): 35-39.

KANDEL, D. B., M. DAVIES, and V. H. RAVEIS (1985) "The stressfulness of daily social roles for women." Journal of Health and Social Behavior 26: 64-78.

KANIGEL, R. (1979) "Stay-put Americans." Human Behavior 8: 53-56.

KANTER, R. M. (1977a) Men and Women of the Corporation. New York: Basic Books.

KANTER, R. M. (1977b) Work and Family in the United States: A Critical Review and Agenda for Research and Policy. New York: Russell Sage.

KARP, R. (1985) "The attack on cafeteria plans." Institutional Investor (October): 229-234.

KATZ, M. H. and C. S. PIOTRKOWSKI (1983) "Correlates of family role strain among employed black women." Family Relations 32: 331-339.

KAUFMAN, H. G. (1982) Professionals in Search of Work: Coping with the Stress of Job Loss and Underemployment. New York: John Wiley.

KEITH, P. M. and R. B. SCHAFER (1980) "Role strain and depression in two-job families." Family Relations 29: 483-488.

KELLY, R. F. (1985) "Family policy analysis: The need to integrate qualitative and quantitative research methods." Sociological Methods and Research 13: 363-386.

KELLY, R. F., A. W. SHELDON, and G. L. FOX (1985) "The impact of economic dislocation on the health of children," pp. 94-111 in J. Boulet et al. (eds.) Understanding the Economic Crisis. Ann Arbor: University of Michigan.

KELLY, R. F. and P. VOYDANOFF (1985) "Work/family role strain among employed parents." Family Relations 34: 367-374.

KERACHSKY, S., W. NICHOLSON, E. CAVIN, and A. HERSHEY (1986) "Work sharing programs: an evaluation of their use." Monthly Labor Review (May): 31-33.

KING, C. (1982) The Social Impacts of Mass Layoff. Ann Arbor: Center for Research on Social Organization, University of Michigan.

KINGSTON, P. W. and S. L. NOCK (1985) "Consequences of the family work day." Journal of Marriage and the Family 47: 619-629.

KLEIN, D. (1983) "Trends in employment and unemployment in families." Monthly Labor Review (December): 21-25.

KOHN, M. L. (1977) Class and Conformity. Chicago: University of Chicago Press.

KOHN, M. L. and C. SCHOOLER (1983) Work and Personality: An Inquiry Into the Impact of Social Stratification. Norwood, NJ: Ablex.

KOMAROVSKY, M. (1940) The Unemployed Man and His Family. New York: Dryden.

KRAUSE, N. and S. STRYKER (1980) "Job-related stress, economic stress, and psycho-physiological well-being." Presented at the Annual Meeting of the North Central Sociological Association, Dayton, OH.

LARSON, J. H. (1984) "The effect of husband's unemployment on marital and family relations in blue-collar families." Family Relations 33 (October): 503-511.

LEE, R. A. (1983) "Flextime and conjugal roles." Journal of Occupational Behavior 5: 297-315.

LEIN, L. (1979) "Male participation in home life." Family Coordinator 28: 489-495.

LEVENTMAN, P. G. (1981) Professionals Out of Work. New York: Free Press.

LICHTER, D. T. (1983) "Socioeconomic returns to migration among married women." Social Forces 62: 487-503.

LIEBOW, E. (1967) Tally's Corner. Boston: Little Brown.

LIEM, R. (1985) "Unemployment: a family as well as a personal crisis," pp. 112-118 in J. Boulet et al. (eds.) Understanding the Economic Crisis. Ann Arbor: University of Michigan.

LIKER, J. K. and G. H. ELDER, Jr. (1983) "Economic hardship and marital relations in the 1930s." American Sociological Review 48: 343-359.

LUPRI, E. (1984) "Comments—bringing women back in," pp. 78-87 in M. B. Brinkerhoff (ed.) Family and Work: Comparative Convergences. Westport, CT: Greenwood.

MARGOLIS, D. (1979) The Managers: Corporate Life in America. New York: Morrow.

MARGOLIS, L. H. (1982) Helping the Families of Unemployed Workers. Chapel Hill: University of North Carolina Press.

MARKHAM, W. T. and J. H. PLECK (1986) "Sex and willingness to move for occupational advancement." Sociological Quarterly 27: 121-143.

MARKS, S. R. (1977) "Multiple roles and role strain." American Sociological Review 42: 921-936.

MARSHALL, G. (1984) "On the sociology of women's unemployment, its neglect and significance." Sociological Review 32: 234-259.

MASNICK, G. and M. J. BANE (1980) The Nation's Families: 1960-1990. Cambridge, MA: Joint Center for Urban Studies of MIT and Harvard University.

McALLISTER, R., E. BUTLER, and E. KAISER (1973) "The adjustment of women to residential mobility." Journal of Marriage and the Family 35: 197-204.

McCUBBIN, H. I., C. B. JOY, A. E. CAUBLE, J. K. COMEAU, J. M. PATTERSON, and R. H. NEEDLE (1980) "Family stress and coping: decade review." Journal of Marriage and the Family 42: 855-871.

McLAUGHLIN, S. D. (1982) "Differential patterns of female labor-force participation surrounding the first birth." Journal of Marriage and the Family 44: 407-420.

McLEAN, A. A. (1979) Work Stress. Reading, MA: Addison-Wesley.

MILLER, J. (1980) "Individual and occupational determinants of job satisfaction." Sociology of Work and Occupations 7: 337-366.

MILLER, J. and H. H. GARRISON (1982) "Sex roles: the division of labor at home and in the workplace." Annual Review of Sociology 8: 237-262.

MILLER, J., C. SCHOOLER, M. KOHN, and K. MILLER (1979) "Women and work: the psychological effects of occupational conditions." American Journal of Sociology 85: 66-94.

MILLER, S. J. (1976) "Family life cycle, extended family orientations, and economic aspirations as factors in the propensity to migrate." Sociological Quarterly 17: 323-335.

MOEN, P. (1979) "Family impacts of the 1975 recession: duration of unemployment." Journal of Marriage and the Family 41: 561-572.

MOEN, P. and M. MOOREHOUSE (1983) "Overtime over the life cycle: a test of the life cycle squeeze hypothesis," pp. 201-218 in H. Z. Lopata and J. H. Pleck (eds.) Research in the Interweave of Social Roles: Family and Jobs, vol. 3. Greenwich, CT: JAI.

MOONEY, M. (1981) "Wives' permanent employment and husbands' hours of work." Industrial Relations 20: 205-211.

MOORE, J. M. (1981) "Relocation policy update." Personnel Administrator (December): 39-42.

MOORE, K. A. and S. L. HOFFERTH (1979) "Effects of women's employment on marriage: formation, stability and roles." Marriage and Family Review 2: 27-36.

MOORE, K. A. and I. V. SAWHILL (1984) "Implications of women's employment for home and family life," in P. Voydanoff (ed.) Work and Family: Changing Roles of Men and Women. Palo Alto, CA: Mayfield.

MOORE, K. A., D. SPAIN, and S. BIANCHI (1984) "Working wives and mothers," pp. 77-98 in B. B. Hess and M. B. Sussman (eds.) Women and the Family: Two Decades of Change. New York: Haworth.

MORTIMER, J. T. (1980) "Occupation-family linkages as perceived by men in the early stages of professional and managerial careers," pp. 99-117 in Research in the Interweave of Social Roles, vol. 1. Women and Men. Greenwich, CT: JAI.

MORTIMER, J. T., R. HALL, and R. HILL (1978) "Husbands' occupational attributes as constraints on wives' employment." Sociology of Work and Occupations 5: 285-313.

MORTIMER, J. T. and G. SORENSEN (1984) "Men, women, work, and family," pp. 139-167 in K. M. Borman et al. (eds.) Women in the Workplace: Effects on Families. Norwood, NJ: Ablex.

MOTT, P. E., F. C. MANN, Q. McLOUGHLIN, and D. P. WARWICK (1965) Shift Work. Ann Arbor: University of Michigan Press.

NARDONE, T. J. (1986) "Part-time workers: who are they?" Monthly Labor Review (February): 13-19.

NATHANSON, C. A. (1980) "Social roles and health status among women: the significance of employment." Social Science and Medicine 14A: 463-471.

NOLLEN, S. D. (1982) New Work Schedules in Practice. New York: Van Nostrand Reinhold.

NORTON, A. J. (1983) "Family life cycle: 1980." Journal of Marriage and the Family 45: 267-275.

NORTON, A. J. and P. C. GLICK (1986) "One parent families: a social and economic profile." Family Relations 35: 9-17.

NOWAK, T. C. and K. A. SNYDER (1984) "Job loss, marital happiness, and household tension." Presented at the Annual Meeting of the Society for the Study of Social Problems, San Antonio, TX.

OPPENHEIMER, V. K. (1982) Work and the Family: A Study in Social Demography. New York: Academic.

OWEN, J. D. (1976) "Workweeks and leisure: an analysis of trends, 1948-75." Monthly Labor Review (August): 3-8.

PACKARD, V. (1972) A Nation of Strangers. New York: David McKay.

PAPANEK, H. (1973) "Men, women and work: reflections on the two-person career." American Journal of Sociology 78: 852-872.

PAPANEK, H. (1979) "Family status production." Signs 7: 775-781.

PARSONS, T. (1949) "The social structure of the family," pp. 241-274 in R. Anshen (ed.) The Family: Its Function and Destiny. New York: Harper.

PARSONS, T. (1955) "The stability of the American family system," pp. 3-9 in T. Parsons and R. F. Bales (eds.) Family, Socialization and Interaction Process. New York: Free Press.

PAULSON, N. (1982) "Change in family income position: the effect of wife's labor force participation." Sociological Focus 15: 77-91.

PEARLIN, L. I., M. A. LIEBERMAN, E. MENAGHAN, and J. T. MULLAN (1981) "The stress process." Journal of Health and Social Behavior 19: 18-26.

PEARLIN, L. I. and C. SCHOOLER (1978) "The structure of coping." Journal of Health and Social Behavior 19: 18-26.

PERRUCCI, C. C., R. PERRUCCI, D. B. TARG, and H. R. TARG (1985) "Impact of a plant closing on workers and the community," in I. H. Simpson and R. L. Simpson (eds.) Research in the Sociology of Work: A Research Annual, vol. III. Greenwich, CT: JAI.

PESKIN, J. (1982) "Measuring household production for the GNP." Family Economics Review (Summer): 16-25.

PETT, M. A. and B. VAUGHAN-COLE (1986) "The impact of income issues and social status on post-divorce adjustment of custodial parents." Family Relations 35: 103-111.

PHILLIBER, W. W. and D. V. HILLER (1983) "Relative occupational attainments of spouses and later changes in marriage and wife's work experience." Journal of Marriage and the Family 45: 161-170.

PIOTRKOWSKI, C. S. (1979) Work and the Family System. New York: Free Press.

PIOTRKOWSKI, C. S. and P. CRITS-CHRISTOPH (1981) "Women's jobs and family adjustment." Journal of Family Issues 2: 126-147.

PLECK, E. (1976) "Two worlds in one: work and family." Journal of Social History 10: 178-195.

PLECK, J. H. (1977a) "Developmental stages in men's lives: how do they differ from women's?" Presented at the conference on Resocialization of Sex Roles: Challenge for the 1970's, Hartland, MI.

PLECK, J. H. (1977b) "The work-family role system." Social Problems 24: 417-428.

PLECK, J. H. (1979) "Work-family conflict: a national assessment." Presented at the Annual Meeting of the Society for the Study of Social Problems, Boston.

PLECK, J. H. (1983) "Husband's paid work and family roles: current research issues," pp. 251-333 in H. Z. Lopata and J. H. Pleck (eds.) Research in the Interweave of Social Roles: Families and Jobs, vol. 3. Greenwich, CT: JAI.

PLECK, J. H. (1986) "Employment and fatherhood: issues and innovative policies," in M. E. Lamb (ed.) The Father's Role: Applied Pespectives. New York: Wiley-Interscience.

PLECK, J. H. and L. LANG (1978) "Men's family role." Unpublished manuscript.

PLECK, J. H. and G. L. STAINES (1985) "Work schedules and family life in two-earner couples." Journal of Family Issues 6: 61-82.

POWELL, D. H., and P. F. DRISCOLL (1973) "Middle-class professionals face unemployment." Society 10: 18-26.

QUARM, D. (1984) "Sexual inequality: the high cost of leaving parents to women," pp. 187-208 in K. M. Borman et al. (eds.) Women in the Workplace: Effects on Families. Norwood, NJ: Ablex.

QUINN, R. P. and G. L. STAINES (1979) The 1977 Quality of Employment Survey. Ann Arbor: University of Michigan.

RALLINGS, E. M. and F. I. NYE (1979) "Wife-mother employment, family, and society," in W. R. Burr et al. (eds.) Contemporary Theories about the Family, vol. I. New York: Free Press.

RAPOPORT, R., R. RAPOPORT, and V. THIESSEN (1974) "Couple symmetry and enjoyment." Journal of Marriage and the Family 36: 588-591.

RAYMAN, P. (1983) "Out of work: the effects of urban unemployment." Unpublished manuscript, Brandeis University.

RENSHAW, J. R. (1976) "An exploration of the dynamics of the overlapping worlds of work and family." Family Process 15: 143-165.

RESKIN, B. F. and H. I. HARTMANN [eds.] (1986) Women's Work, Men's Work: Sex Segregation on the Job. Washington, DC: National Academy Press.

RODMAN, H. (1971) Lower-Class Families. New York: Oxford University Press.

RODMAN, H., and C. SAFILIOS-ROTHSCHILD (1983) "Weak links in men's worker-earner roles: a descriptive model," pp. 219-238 in Research in the Interweave of Social Roles: Jobs and Families, vol. 3. Greenwich, CT: JAI.

ROOS, P. A. (1983) "Marriage and women's occupational attainment in cross-cultural perspective." American Sociological Review 48: 852-864.

ROOT, K. (1984) "The human response to plant closures." Annals of the American Academy of Political and Social Science 475: 52-65.

ROOT, K. (1977) "Workers and their families in a plant shutdown." Presented at the Annual Meeting of the American Sociological Association.

ROSENFELD, R. A. (1979) "Women's occupational careers." Sociology of Work and Occupations 6: 283-311.

RUBIN, L. B. (1976) Worlds of Pain: Life in the Working-Class Family. New York: Basic Books.

SANDEFUR, G. D. (1985) "Variations in interstate migration of men across the early stages of the life cycle." Demography 22: 353-366.

SANIK, M. and T. MAULDIN (1986) "Single versus two parent families: a comparison of mothers' time." Family Relations 35: 53-56.

SCANZONI, J. (1970) Opportunity and the Family. New York: Free Press.

SCANZONI, J. (1982) Sexual Bargaining. Chicago: Univeristy of Chicago.

SCANZONI, L. and J. SCANZONI (1981) Men, Women and Change. New York: McGraw-Hill.

SCHERVISH, P. G. (1985) "Family life and the economy." Presented at the video teleconference, "The Bishops' Pastoral Letter on the Economy and Its Relationship to Family Life," Loyola University, Chicago.

SCHLOZMAN, K. L. (1979) "Women and unemployment: assessing the biggest myths," pp. 290-312 in J. Freeman (ed.) Women: A Feminist Perspective. Palo Alto, CA: Mayfield.

SEHGAL, E. (1984) "Work experience in 1983 reflects the effects of the recovery." Monthly Labor Review (December): 18-24.

SEIDENBERG, R. (1973) Corporate Wives—Corporate Casualties? New York: AMACOM.

SELL, R. R. (1983) "Transferred jobs: a neglected aspect of migration and occupational change." Work & Occupations 10: 179-206.

SHAMIR, B. (1985) "Sex differences in psychological adjustment to unemployment." Social Problems 33: 67-79.

SHANK, S. E. (1985) "Employment rose in the first half of 1985 as the recovery entered its third year." Monthly Labor Review (August): 3-8.

SHANK, S. E. and P. M. GETZ (1986) "Employment and unemployment: developments in 1985." Monthly Labor Review (February): 3-12.

SHAW, L. B. (1982) Unplanned Careers: The Working Lives of Middle-Aged Women. Lexington, MA: D. C. Heath.

SHOSTAK, A. B. (1980) Blue-Collar Stress. Reading, MA: Addison-Wesley.

SIDDIQUE, C. M. (1981) "Orderly careers and social integration." Industrial Relations 20: 297-305.

SIEBER, S. D. (1974) "Toward a theory of role accumulation." American Sociological Review 39: 567-578.

SLOTE, A. (1969) Termination: The Closing at Baker Plant. New York: Bobbs-Merrill.

SMITH, S. J. (1982) "New worklife estimates reflect changing profile of labor force." Monthly Labor Review 105 (March): 15-20.

SMITH, S. J. (1983) "Estimating annual hours of labor force activity." Monthly Labor Review 106 (February): 13-22.

SMITH, S. J. (1986) "Work experience profile, 1984: the effects of recovery continue." Monthly Labor Review (February): 37-45.

SMITH-LOVIN, L. and A. R. TICKAMYER (1978) "Nonrecursive models of labor force participation, fertility behavior and sex role attitudes." American Sociological Review 43: 541-557.

SORENSEN, A. (1983) "Women's employment patterns after marriage." Journal of Marriage and the Family 45: 311-321.

SPITZE, G. (1984) "The effect of family migration on wives' employment: how long does it last?" Social Science Quarterly 65: 21-36.

SPITZE, G. (1986) "Family migration largely unresponsive to wife's employment (across age groups)." Sociology and Social Research 70: 231-234.

SPITZE, G. and S. J. SOUTH (1985) "Women's employment, time expenditure, and divorce." Journal of Family Issues 6: 307-329.

ST. JOHN-PARSONS, D. (1978) "Continuous dual-career families." Psychology of Women Quarterly 3: 30-42.

STACK, C. B. (1974) All Our Kin. New York: Harper.

STAFFORD, F. and G. J. DUNCAN (1979) "The use of time and technology by households in the United States." Working paper, Institute for Social Research, University of Michigan.

STAINES, G. L. and J. H. PLECK (1983) The Impact of Work Schedules on the Family. Ann Arbor: University of Michigan Press.

STEINBERG, L. D., R. CATALANO, and D. DOOLEY (1981) "Economic antecedents of child abuse and neglect." Child Development 52: 975-985.

STEINER, J. (1972) "What price success?" Harvard Business Review 50: 69-74.

SUSSMAN, M. B. and B. E. COGSWELL (1971) "Family influences on job movement." Human Relations 24: 477-487.

SUTER, L. E. and H. P. MILLER (1973) "Income differences between men and career women." American Journal of Sociology 78: 962-974.

SWEETLAND, J. (1979) Occupational Stress and Productivity. Scarsdale, NY: Work in America Institute.

SZINOVACZ, M. E. (1984) "Changing family roles and interactions," pp. 163-201 in B. B. Hess and M. B. Sussman (eds.) Women and the Family: Two Decades of Change. New York: Haworth Press.

TAYLOR, D. E. and E. S. SEKSCENSKI (1982) "Workers on long schedules, single and multiple jobholders." Monthly Labor Review (May): 47-53.

THOITS, P. A. (1983) "Multiple identities and psychological well-being." American Sociological Review 48: 174-187.

TIGER, L. (1974) "Is this trip necessary? The heavy human costs of moving executives around." Fortune (September): 139-141.

TILLY, L. A. (1979) "Individual lives and family strategies in the French Proletariat." Journal of Family History 4: 137-152.

TOGNOLI, J. (1979) "The flight from domestic space: men's roles in the household." Family Coordinator 28: 599-607.

Urban League Review (1976) "The myth of income cushions during the 1974-75 depression." Vol. 2, pp. 43-53.

U.S. Bureau of the Census (1983) Geographic Mobility of Labor, March 1980 to March 1981. Current Population Reports Series P-20, no. 377. Washington, DC: U.S. Department of Commerce.

U.S. Commission on Civil Rights (1981) Child Care and Equal Opportunity for Women. Washington, DC: U.S. Commission on Civil Rights.

U.S. Commission on Civil Rights (1983) A Growing Crisis: Disadvantaged Women and Their Children. Washington, DC: U.S. Commission on Civil Rights.

VAN MAANEN, J. (1977) "Summary: towards a theory of the career," pp. 161-179 in J. Van Maanen (ed.) Organizational Careers. New York: John Wiley.

VANEK, J. (1974) "Time spent on housework." Scientific American 231, 5: 116-120.

VERBRUGGE, L. M. (1983) "Multiple roles and physical health of women and men." Journal of Health and Social Behavior 24: 16-30.

VERBRUGGE, L. M. (1985) "Role burdens and physical health of women and men." Presented at the Annual Meeting of the American Sociological Association, Washington, DC.

VOYDANOFF, P. (1982) "Work roles and quality of family life among professionals and managers." pp. 118-124 in B. M. Hirschlein and W. J. Braun (eds.) Families and Work. Stillwater: Oklahoma State University Press.

VOYDANOFF, P. (1984a) "Economic distress and families: policy issues." Journal of Family Issues 5: 273-288.

VOYDANOFF, P. (1984b) "Work role characteristics, family structure demands and quality of family life." Paper presented at the Annual Meeting of the National Council on Family Relations.

VOYDANOFF, P. and B. W. DONNELLY (1986a) Economic Distress and Mental Health. Final report submitted to the Ohio Department of Mental Health.

VOYDANOFF, P. and B. W. DONNELLY (1986b) "Economic distress and mental health: the role of coping resources and behaviors." Presented at the Annual Meeting of the American Sociological Association, New York.

VOYDANOFF, P. and B. W. DONNELLY (forthcoming) "Economic distress, family coping, and quality of family life," in P. Voydanoff and L. C. Majka (eds.) Families and Economic Distress: Coping Strategies and Social Policy. Beverly Hills, CA: Sage.

VOYDANOFF, P. and R. F. KELLY (1984) "Determinants of work-related family problems among employed parents." Journal of Marriage and the Family 46: 881-892.

WAITE, L. J., G. W. HAGGSTROM, and D. E. KANOUSE (1985) "Changes in the employment activities of new parents." American Sociological Review 50: 263-272.

WALDMAN, E. (1983) "Labor force statistics from a family perspective." Monthly Labor Review (December): 16-20.

WALDMAN, E., A. S. GROSSMAN, H. HAYGHE, and B. L. JOHNSON (1979) "Working mothers in the 1970's: a look at the statistics." Monthly Labor Review (October): 39-49.

WARR, P. (1984) "Job loss, unemployment and psychological well-being," pp. 263-285 in V. L. Allen and E. van de Vliert (eds.) Role transitions. New York: Plenum.

WEISS, R. S. (1984) "The impact of marital dissolution on income and consumption in single-parent households." Journal of Marriage and the Family 46: 115-127.

WEITZMAN, L. J. (1985) The Divorce Revolution. New York: Free Press.

White House Conference on Families (1980) Listening to America's Families. Washington, DC: Author.

WILENSKY, H. (1961) "Orderly careers and social participation." American Sociological Review 26: 521-539.

WILKIE, J. R. (1981) "The trend toward delayed parenthood." Journal of Marriage and the Family 43: 583-591.

WINETT, R. A. and M. S. NEALE (1980) "Modifying settings as a strategy for permanent, preventive behavior change," pp. 407-437 in P. Karoly and J. J. Steffan (eds.) Improving the Long-Term Effects of Psychotherapy. New York: Gardner.

WOODS, N. F. and B. S. HULKA (1979) "Symptom reports and illness behavior among employed women and homemakers." Journal of Community Health 5: 36-45.

YOUNG, M. and P. WILLMOTT (1973) The Symmetrical Family. New York: Penguin Books.

ZALUSKY, J. (1978) "Shiftwork—complex of problems." AFL-CIO Federationist (May): 1-6.

Author Index

Subject Index

About the Author

Patricia Voydanoff is Director of the Center for the Study of Family Development at the University of Dayton. She received a bachelor's degree in psychology from Ohio Wesleyan University, a master's degree in sociology and industrial relations from Wayne State University, and a doctoral degree in sociology from Wayne State University. She has authored *The Implications of Work-Family Relationships for Productivity* (Work in American Institute, 1980), edited *Work and Family: Changing Roles of Men and Women* (Mayfield Publishing, 1984), coedited *The Changing Family: Reflections on Familiaris Consortio* (Loyola University Press, 1984), and is coediting *Families and Economic Distress: Coping Strategies and Social Policy* (Sage Publications, forthcoming). Her research on the work and family roles of men and women and the effects of economic distress on families has been published in numerous scholarly journals.